Praise for Marc D. Angel's *A New*

I don't know whether Rabbi Marc Angel's mother was right in assuming that "we could learn almost everything we need to know about human nature from our own extended family," but I would go as far as to claim that we could learn almost everything we need to know about Sephardic ethos and way of life from Rabbi Angel's reminiscences. And we certainly should. For our own sake! Out of many faces that Judaism developed, the Sephardic one still radiates as the most "equilibric" one.

— Dr. Eliezer Papo, Chairman of the Moshe David Gaon Center for Ladino Culture at Ben-Gurion University of the Negev

This memoir of growing up in a close-knit Sephardic immigrant community is poignant and a pleasure to read. It's also sharp and provocative. It pushes us to figure out how, in our vexed, complicated world today, we can provide our children with a natural sense of belonging and joy.

— Jane Mushabac, CUNY Professor of English, author of *His Hundred Years, A Tale*

A beautiful family memoir and an unforgettable contribution to Sephardic-American letters… a window on the little-known world of Seattle's Sephardic Jews.

— Jonathan D. Sarna, Brandeis University and author of *American Judaism: A History*

Rabbi Angel's absorbing memoir of growing-up in Seattle, Washington, is an ode to the Ottoman-Sephardic culture and Judeo-Spanish language in which he was raised. Though it has gradually faded among subsequent generations, its beauty and lasting meaning, too valuable to lose, is the main thrust of the book. In each chapter—whether he has recounted an event, religious tradition, folk remedy, humor, adages, even food and music—the author points out a life lesson, a human value, and a relevance for today.

— Rachel Amado Bortnick, Founder of Ladinokomunita

In a creative blend of narrative, nostalgia and personal memoir, Rabbi Marc. D. Angel transports us back to the once-upon-a-time world of the Ladino-Sephardic community of his upbringing in Seattle, where Sephardic immigrants seamlessly blended religion, family traditions from the old country and modern-day values to create a joyous and uplifting Jewish way of life, one that could still serve as a model to emulate for our communities today.

— Rabbi Daniel Bouskila, International Director of the Sephardic Educational Center

A New World

An American Sephardic Memoir

MARC D. ANGEL

Albion
Andalus
Boulder, Colorado
2019

*"The old shall be renewed,
and the new shall be made holy."*
— Rabbi Avraham Yitzhak Kook

Albion-Andalus, Inc.
P. O. Box 19852
Boulder, CO 80308
www.albionandalus.com

Design and composition by Erica Holland Leitz
Cover design by D.A.M. Cool Graphics
Cover image of Marco and Sultana Romey (author's maternal grandparents) with their children.

Manufactured in the United States of America

ISBN-10: 1-7336589-2-0

ISBN-13: 978-1-7336589-2-8

We thank the Institute for Jewish Ideas and Ideals and the Sephardic Educational Center for their support of this publication as part of their "Sephardic Initiative."

Contents

Preface

Transitions.

Things stay the same, but not really. Things change, but not totally.

My grandparents were among the 30,000 or so Sephardic Jews who came to the United States during the early 20th century. They were born and raised in Turkey and the Island of Rhodes. They had little formal education, little money, but a lot of courage.

They brought the "old country" with them to the new world. Their language was Judeo-Spanish. Their culture was the traditional Sephardic Judaism of Ottoman Jewry. They settled in Seattle, Washington, and were part of a vibrant Sephardic enclave with large extended families.

My grandparents were of the "old world" and they sought to transmit their ideals and values to their children. Their children were of the "new world." Life in America was very different from the tradition-centered life of the Jews in Turkey and Rhodes. The children's generation respected their parents; but this new American generation was restless. They wanted to adapt fully to American life. How much of the "old world" could they carry with them? How much of it had to be left behind?

By my generation (I was born in 1945), the Americanization process was well advanced. We loved and admired our grandparents and their generation; but we were full-blooded Americans, many of us with American-born parents. The "old world" was remote, somewhat exotic. It didn't define who we were.

Our children and grandchildren are further removed from the "old country." Most have never heard a conversation in Judeo-Spanish. Most have not had personal contact with members of my grandparents' generation.

The Americanization of our family over the past hundred years has brought many changes. We are far better educated than the immigrant generation. We are generally more affluent, more "successful," and more integrated into American society. We have shared in the American dream.

But we have also incurred losses in the generational transitions. Life is not static. Things change. Circumstances change. People change. Whereas most of our family once lived within the same neighborhood in Seattle, now we are spread out all over the country. Whereas most of our family once felt a strong sense of belonging to the Sephardic Jewish tradition, now we are much more diverse in our religious and cultural patterns of life.

While we can't go back to the "old days" and the "old country" way of life, we can draw meaningful lessons for ourselves and our next generations. In assembling the memoirs for this book, I have chosen people and events that have left a lasting impression on me…and that I think can leave a lasting impression on many others. This book is one man's record of an era which is rapidly coming to a close. I acknowledge that memoirs are subjective; each person experiences life through his or her own eyes and each remembers things differently.

I thank my wife, Gilda, for her wisdom, enthusiasm…and love. She read the manuscript of this book with great insight and made important editorial contributions to it. I express my gratitude to Netanel Miles-Yépez of Albion-Andalus Books for believing in this book and seeing it to publication. And I thank the Almighty for having brought me to this day.

Part I

Beginnings

My mother used to say that we could learn almost everything we need to know about human nature from our own extended family. Some relatives were wise, some foolish; some were successful, some failures; some optimistic, some morose; some pious, some rebellious. Our family included intellectuals and people of very limited intelligence. We had courageous and outspoken individuals, and we had timid, quiet types. Some had phenomenal senses of humor, and some would hardly ever laugh. In the family, one could experience love, hatred, selflessness, jealousy, greed, generosity, spirituality, materialism, seriousness, humor.

The family included people of great mind and heart, people who were handsome and beautiful, people of striking personality. It also included, without embarrassment, people who were quite ordinary, as well as individuals who had various physical, emotional and mental disabilities.

My grandfather Angel had a shoeshine stand. My grandfather Romey was a barber. My father was a grocer. Among my uncles were a butcher, fish salesman, rabbi, printer, storekeeper, bartender, college professor, and assorted unskilled laborers. Various relatives were real estate speculators, never-do-wells, while others were employees of Boeing. In the days of my childhood, most of the women of our family did not work outside the home.

By the next generation, the extended family came to include

rabbis, teachers, attorneys, insurance and real estate agents, a political scientist, skilled employees in various companies, a merchant marine, salespeople, athletes, a nurse, and several authors of books.

My mother saw the family as something of a microcosm of humanity in general and society in particular. We could understand the world around us if we could understand ourselves.

In those days, the family was large, diverse and whole. We mostly lived in the same neighborhood; we got together often; we recognized a strong vital sense of kinship among ourselves.

One of the focal points of my childhood was the home of my maternal grandparents at 214 15th Avenue in Seattle, Washington. Even now, so many years after their deaths, I often find myself reminiscing about that house, remembering so many details about it. It has stood as a symbol in my mind of our family together. It calls to mind a simpler time, a time when life seemed whole and connected.

A number of years ago, my wife and children and I were visiting Seattle. Whenever we were in town, we took a drive through the "old neighborhood," including a stop at my grandparents' house. But this time, as we pulled up in front of 214 15th Avenue, we found the windows of the house boarded up. The grass in the large yard had not been cut in months. A sign on the front door stated that the house had been condemned.

It struck me that the house might be torn down. It also struck me that the family togetherness which that house had symbolized for me was also in the process of coming apart. Indeed, our family now had members living in different parts of the country (my own family lived in New York City). We had divorced people; we had individuals who had forsaken our family religious traditions. Even the family members who still lived in Seattle were spread out in different neighborhoods of the city and suburbs. If my grandparents' house had become a ghostlike edifice, so the image of our family during the years of my childhood also had become a ghostlike memory.

Fortunately, as I learned some time later, my grandparents'

house was not destroyed after all. A family bought it and restored it.

And fortunately, our extended family still exists on some level. From time to time, family members make an effort to bring back bits of the feelings from the old days.

But neither the old house nor our family are really the same anymore. And no one can put the pieces together again. A civilization has passed forever.

I decided to put down a few memories and observations as a way of conveying the spirit of that civilization. I share Mom's belief that the extended family was a microcosm of society. Although this book talks about my extended family during the years of my childhood in Seattle (1945-1963), it in fact is speaking about a facet of immigrant American society that a great many American families shared. And lost.

This book is a collection of my memories. It is the past sifted through the prism of my own mind. So in a real sense, this book is my personal story. At the same time, though, it is a story that has relevance to a great many people who are rooted in traditional societies, and who strive to adapt to an ever-changing modern world. The story is unique…and universal.

My father, Victor Angel, was born in Seattle, April 1, 1913. My mother, Rachel Romey Angel, was born in Seattle, December 28, 1914.

But even these seemingly straightforward facts are embroiled in controversy.

Dad was born at home, not in a hospital. His parents, immigrants from the Island of Rhodes, were not too fussy about registering his birth and obtaining a birth certificate for him. He was definitely born, that was a fact; what difference would it make if his birth were recorded in the government files?

My grandfather, Bohor Yehudah Angel, had come to Seattle in 1908, following his eldest son Moshe who had come a bit earlier. The two of them operated a shoeshine stand and saved enough money to send for the rest of the family. My grandmother, Bulissa Huniu Angel, arrived in the United States in 1911 with her children Ralph, Victoria, Luna, Avner, Joseph and Rahamim. Joseph, who was then about nine or ten years old, was turned away by immigration officials since he had a contagious scalp disease (tinias). He was sent back to Rhodes and lived with relatives there. Although I never knew Uncle Joseph, his life's story hovered over our family's collective memory.

My father was the first and only American-born child in the family.

Like the rest of his family, he spoke Judeo-Spanish as his mother tongue. This was the language of Sephardic Jews whose ancestors had been expelled from Catholic Spain in 1492. Though born in the United States, my father did not learn English until he went to public school at age five.

When registering him for school, his parents were asked for his birth date. In the old country, birth dates were not that important. Generally, people would know that they were born in "the year of the big flood," of "the year of the drought," or by some other unusual phenomenon. As to the month in the year, they would know that they were born "around Rosh haShanah," or "before Purim," or in connection with some other Jewish holy day.

My grandparents told the school officials that my father's birthday was April 1. Who could refute them? Many years later, when Dad applied for a passport, he had to demonstrate proof of birth. I was then a student in college and decided to confront the bureaucracy by obtaining a genuine birth certificate for him. We first asked the birth certificate office in Olympia (Washington's State Capital) to search for a record of Dad's birth. None turned up. We then provided various documents in which Dad had listed his birth date as April 1, 1913. We also obtained testimonial letters from two elders who would swear that April 1, 1913 was the correct date. After submitting this material, we waited patiently. It was not long before my father received a real birth certificate. We congratulated him on obtaining proof that he had been born. His existence was now official.

My mother's birth date was tied to a different sort of problem.

Her parents had come to Seattle as teenagers. My grandfather, Marco Romey, born in Tekirdag, Turkey, arrived in Seattle in 1908. My grandmother, Sultana Policar Romey, arrived in 1911. She had been born on the Island of Marmara, a Turkish island in the Sea of Marmara. She had come to Seattle at the request of her older sister, Calo, who had settled in Seattle several years earlier. Calo was sure that her younger sister would have a better life in America than in her poverty stricken village of Marmara.

My grandparents Romey were married in Seattle in May 1912. My mother was the second of their seven children. As she grew up, they told her that her birthday was January 7. That is the date she celebrated throughout her childhood and for many years thereafter. When she grew older and applied for her passport, she wrote away to get a copy of her birth certificate. When she received it, she was surprised to find that her birthday was not listed as January 7, 1915, but as December 28, 1914. Mom solved the discrepancy by declaring that she no longer had a birthday— but rather a birthday week. After her birth certificate came in, we celebrated her birthday every year from December 28 to January 7.

Mom died on May 28, 1983. Dad died on July 28, 1991. They are buried side by side in the Sephardic cemetery in Seattle. There are no controversies about the dates of their deaths.

My parents often told us that they were members of a transition generation. Their parents had been born and raised in the old country, having come to Seattle as immigrants. Although the newcomers had certainly made efforts to Americanize, they were very much steeped in the old world culture. My grandfather Romey learned to read and write English; he spoke English uncomfortably, much preferring his mother tongue, Judeo-Spanish. He became an American citizen. My other grandparents only learned enough English to understand what their grandchildren said to them. They spoke English poorly, and never became United States citizens. My grandmother Romey would say that although she had arrived in Seattle as a teenager, she was never able to give up feeling that her real home was in Marmara, that she was in Seattle only on a temporary basis. She made as few concessions to American culture as she could.

As immigrants, my grandparents brought with them the memories and traditions of their families in Rhodes and Turkey. They conducted their households and family life along the models that they had experienced in the old country. My mother used to say: "I might just as well have been born in Turkey. I feel that I, too, am a sort of immigrant in the United States even though I was born here."

But my parents' children were the other side of the transition. We were English-speaking, full-blooded Americans. We went on to become college educated, professional, mobile, and modern. We were two generations removed from the old world. We were part of the generation that was totally comfortable in America, without a sense of being immigrants or foreigners.

Mom and Dad spoke Judeo-Spanish to their parents and to their parents' generation. They spoke English to their children and their children's generation. To each other, they used both languages, a blend of the languages, a jumping from one language to the other; but English predominated.

In the last months of Mom's life, I found that she was speaking to me more and more in Judeo-Spanish. She sang some of the old songs, used some of the old proverbs and expressions. I think she died in Judeo-Spanish. In the last months of Dad's life, I don't recall him reverting to Judeo-Spanish. He had survived my mother's death by eight years and had few people with whom he could use the old language. He died in English.

My parents, both born in Seattle, still had living memories and connections with the old world. Their minds and spirits were animated by the civilization of their parents and ancestors. They spoke the same language, ate the same foods, and shared the same cultural and religious patterns. They were thoroughly proud Americans; but their souls were nurtured in the Sephardic civilization of Turkey and Rhodes.

My grandparents' generation, the generation of immigrants, has passed away. My parents' generation, the generation of transition, has almost completely died out.

And my generation, the generation of pure Americans, is still trying to understand its connection with its past. We also have an old country. We also have memories that inspirit our lives. We also hear the voices of ancestors. But the old country is different for us.

My old country is Seattle.

I was born July 25, 1945, the second of four children born to my parents.

According to the practice of the Sephardic Jews of Turkey and Rhodes, children are named according to a traditional pattern: the first-born boy and girl are named after the father's parents, and the second-born boy and girl are named after the mother's parents. Subsequent children are named for other relatives, alternating from the father's to the mother's side of the family.

This custom underscores the strong family ties inculcated by Sephardic culture. Each child, by his and her very name, is placed into a context. The newborn already has a history, a tradition. Often enough, he or she is named after a grandparent who is still alive. The grandparents witness their continuity in the persons of their grandchildren. They see little children carrying their own names, marching the family into the future. And the namesakes feel a special bond to the grandparents after whom they were named.

My older brother, the first born, was named Leon Bill. As was proper, he was named after my father's father. My grandfather Angel's name was Yehudah. He was called Bohor Yehudah. (Among Sephardim the first-born child was called by the honorific title "Bohor" for males, and "Bohora" for females.) When it came to naming my brother, my parents chose the name Leon—a commonly used equivalent for Yehudah. Yehudah (Judah) was described in the Bible as a lion. Sephardim used the Judeo-Spanish word for lion i.e. Leon. Since my grandfather was known by the appellation Bohor, that name also had to be included in my brother's name. What was a good, modern American name that began with a "b"? Bill!

So my brother's name tells a story of the new generation in the old country of Seattle. It was faithful to the tradition. He was named after his paternal grandfather. Yet, the names were put into an American framework. After all, it would be much easier for this little Yankee to go through life as Leon Bill than as Bohor Yehudah.

Seven years later, I was born. Being the second-born son, I was named after my maternal grandfather, Marco Romey. My parents thought that Marco sounded too old-fashioned, so they called me Marc. When my third grade teacher asked me why my name was spelled "wrong," since Marc should really end with a "k," I blushed when I told her I had been named after my grandfather Marco. From that day on, and to my youthful embarrassment, she called me Marco.

Of course, I was a full-blooded American so I needed a middle name, even though my grandfather did not have one. Mom decided to distinguish me with the name Dwight, after General Dwight D. Eisenhower. General Eisenhower was then a great hero in the United States, having ended World War II with a striking victory for the allies. In her patriotic fervor, Mom went beyond her Sephardic tradition by naming me for an American war hero. She used to tell me that I was named after two great men: my grandfather Marco Romey and General Dwight Eisenhower. With this combination, I was surely destined for wonderful things!

My sister was born about eighteen months later. As first-born daughter, she was named after her paternal grandmother: Bulissa Esther. Bulissa is a beautiful name but it is definitely not American. My sister became Bernice Esther. In Hebrew, she was called Esther, the "Bulissa" being dropped from this American generation. Certain aspects of a culture can remain intact in the United States; other aspects can be adapted; but some things simply had to be left behind. "Bulissa" was one of those things left behind.

About five and a half years later, my mother gave birth to her fourth and last child. If it had been a girl, she would have been named after my mother's mother, Sultana. Mom had already picked a suitable American version of the name, Sheila. None of us was especially fond of the name Sheila, so we were glad that she gave birth to a boy.

By accepted tradition, the third son should have been named after someone on my father's side. The Angel relatives were aware of this fact and devoted considerable effort lobbying my parents concerning the new child's name. They wanted the boy to be called Joseph, after my father's older brother who had never made it to Seattle and whose family members were murdered by the Nazis in 1944. Mom would not hear of it. She said that Uncle Joseph had been an unfortunate soul "always behind the eight ball." The relatives reversed Mom's logic. They argued that since Joseph had such a miserable life, he deserved at least a posthumous reward—that a child of the family should carry his name.

Who was Uncle Joseph? Why was Mom adamant about not naming her son after him?

In 1911, my grandmother Angel travelled from the Island of Rhodes to America to join her husband and eldest son who had come to Seattle several years earlier. The two men had worked hard to save enough money to bring the rest of the family to America. My grandmother Bulissa undertook the incredibly difficult voyage with six of her children. She also took responsibility to bring a neighbor's daughter to Seattle. She figured that this young lady, Bohora Rosa Capelluto, would be a good wife for her eldest son. And if he did not want to marry her, then perhaps the second son would! (The first-born son, Moshe, did marry her.)

When they arrived in New York, they had to pass through the immigration officials. My grandmother was told that little Joseph could not be admitted into the United States because he had an infectious scalp disease.

What was she to do? She had come half way across the world at great effort and expense. She and her young ones were still three thousand miles away from Seattle. To take them back to Rhodes with Joseph was unthinkable. It would be years before enough money could be raised to again bring them to America. On the other hand, what was she supposed to do with Joseph? How could she abandon her son?

As things turned out, several other Jewish immigrants from Rhodes were also rejected by immigration officials. They told my grandmother that since they were returning to Rhodes, they would bring Joseph back with them. He could be raised temporarily in the home of relatives. When his health improved, he could then be sent on to Seattle.

So my grandmother took five children and a future daughter-in-law to Seattle, tearfully sending her little Joseph back to Rhodes. The separation was heart-rending and never left the consciousness of my grandmother and the rest of the family.

Joseph never did make it to Seattle. He grew up in Rhodes, eventually married and had four children. He stayed in touch with his Seattle family by mail. They sent him money and gifts from time to time. But they never saw each other again.

Among the victims of the barbaric Nazis were almost all of the two thousand Jews living in the Island of Rhodes. My Uncle Joseph's family perished. No one of his family in Rhodes survived. Memorial plaques erected after the war at the Jewish cemetery and on the front wall of the synagogue in Rhodes list the family "Angel" among the victims of the brutal Nazis.

Uncle Joseph's scalp disease that led to his being denied entry into the United States ultimately cost his family their lives. Could the immigration officials who turned him away, separating him from his mother and family, have any idea how much grief they caused the family at that time? And did they ever come to realize that their decision ultimately played a role in the death of that little boy's family?

So, as far as my mother was concerned, the name Joseph was out.

One of Dad's relatives did her best, though, to win this child for the name Joseph. She visited my mother shortly after the baby was born, before he was to be named at the circumcision on the eighth day. With great solemnity and reverence, she told my mother of a vision she had received in a dream the previous night. She was told in the dream that the son of Victor and Rachel Angel would be named Joseph. How could anyone do battle against a vision that came in a dream?

My mother was undaunted. She replied quickly and forcefully. "I also had a dream last night. A vision came to me that this baby should be named David."

"Is that the truth?" asked the elderly relative.

"Yes it is," said my mother with confidence. She had won.

"But David? David? Who is the child being named after? We don't have any David in the Angel family."

My mother said proudly: "I am naming him after King David. I love the name David. He is being named for King David."

Family members were stunned at this unprecedented decision. Children were to be named in a specific pattern, and King David—for all his greatness—was not part of that pattern. My father, in his devotion to my mother, defended her decision. The son would be called David.

To pacify the indignant relatives, my parents agreed to name the child David Victor Joseph Angel. In due course, though, the Joseph was dropped.

The names of my parents' four children are an indication of the immense cultural forces that were sweeping through the Sephardic community of Seattle in our generation. Names describe context. And the family's context was in transition.

Our family lived at 511 28th Avenue, between Jefferson and East Cherry until the fall of 1958. Then we moved to the "new neighborhood" in Seward Park, where we lived at 5602 Wilson Avenue South.

Our house on 28th Avenue was in the central district of Seattle. In those days, it was a fairly mixed area. Most of the city's Jewish population lived in this neighborhood. There were also large numbers of African-Americans, Japanese and Chinese. There were even some WASPs, although few stand out in my memory. By 1958, the neighborhood was in the process of turning into the "Black ghetto."

When we lived on 28th Avenue, before the demographic changes, the neighborhood was a place where we felt a sense of belonging. Almost all of my relatives lived within easy walking distance from our house. Many of the residents of the neighborhood were themselves Sephardic Jews of Turkish and Rhodes origins. I knew I was in a Jewish neighborhood because the language I often heard on the street was Spanish—the unique Spanish of the Sephardic Jews of Turkey and Rhodes.

When I would meet an elder Sephardic Jew who did not know me, I would be asked: "Whose son are you?" I would inform the questioner of my parents' names. Then the person would know exactly who I was, where I came from, how I belonged. We grew up in the community not simply as individuals, but as representatives of a family.

Family was the central factor in our identities in those days. Mom and five of her married siblings and their families all lived in this neighborhood. My grandparents' home at 214 15th Avenue was a focal point of our family life. Most of my father's brothers and sisters—and their children—also lived in the central district. It was difficult to go anywhere in the neighborhood without bumping into a relative or family friend.

The rough boundaries of our world were 31st Avenue to 15th Avenue, from Cherry Street to Yesler Way. Within that area lived dozens of uncles, aunts, cousins, great uncles, great aunts, second cousins, third cousins, people related to us through marriage, people related to our relatives through marriage, people who were not related to us at all but whom we called uncle or aunt out of respect. It seemed to me that we were related to most of the Sephardim in town in one way or another.

The neighborhood included important landmarks: the kosher meat markets, kosher bakeries, the Hebrew Day School, the synagogues, many Jewish businesses. We borrowed books from the Yesler Branch of the Seattle Public Library. We played baseball, flew kites and rode bicycles in the army camp, a big field up the block from our home on 28th Avenue. We went swimming and had picnics at Madrona Park on Lake Washington. Once in a while, we went all the way to Seward Park. Among our favorite outings were trips to Golden Gardens, Salt Water State Park, and Alki.

The neighborhood also had its dangers. First and foremost for us was Pete, the Doberman Pinscher who lived in the lot adjoining our back yard. Pete rarely stopped barking. He often foamed at the mouth. He was chained to his doghouse but had a leeway of about twenty feet. He ran around in circles endlessly, wearing a dirt path in the middle of the yard. The owners obviously did not care. They bought Pete to protect their home from burglars, but how could Pete attack burglars when he was chained to his doghouse in the back yard? I guess they figured that the very sound of Pete's howling would terrify any would-be trespassers.

Pete perpetually appeared to be angry and vicious. From time to time, a ball we were playing with would go over the fence into Pete's territory. If it landed within the dirt circle, we generally gave up on it. No one was willing to invade Pete's province of power. When the ball landed outside the circle, we would venture over the fence to retrieve it. Our logic was that Pete could not go beyond the length of his chain. Even knowing this did not completely remove the terror involved in going into Pete's yard. Usually, one of us would throw dirt bombs in the direction away from where the ball was. Inevitably, Pete would lunge after them. This would give us the chance to send someone—usually we sent my little brother David—to race to the ball and reclaim it.

This system worked for quite a while; but then a flaw developed in our strategy. Pete did what we had never considered possible: he broke his chain. I remember looking out our kitchen window one Sunday morning and not seeing Pete. While puzzling over his absence, we got a call from my Auntie Regina on 27th Avenue that she saw Pete running freely in front of her house. Pete was on the loose.

All our relatives were hastily called and warned. None of us stepped out of our houses in fear of Pete. Later in the day, we saw his owners chaining Pete back to his doghouse. The rumor spread that he had mangled a few dogs during his period of freedom. The fear of Pete increased; rarely would we go into his yard again, even beyond his dirt path circle. Who knew if he would break his chain again?

Shortly before we moved to our new house, Pete once again broke loose. We heard that he tore several dogs to pieces and also attacked some people. The police shot him. Just as our Pete problem came to an end, we moved to our new house in the Seward Park district. We immediately learned that our neighbors, two houses down, owned a dog, Brutus. Brutus was the equal of Pete, only he wasn't kept on a chain!

Homo homini lupus. The old Latin saying describes man as a wolf. The noted psychiatrist, Silvano Arieti, believed that people who feared dogs were actually symbolically expressing a fear of the wolf-like nature of human beings. Perhaps on some level, our experiences with Pete and Brutus reminded us that human society also had its underside, its real dangers.

Even though our old neighborhood was a place where we felt a sense of warmth and belonging, it was also a place where we felt some fears. Not everyone in the neighborhood had nice things to say about Jews. Bigots who didn't even know us would sometimes utter anti-Jewish epithets, reminding us that our security was not complete. We had our share of bullies and trouble makers who kept us on our guard. Some of the hurts that I absorbed in fights in those days continue to hurt me still. The Sephardic author, Elias Canetti, winner of the Nobel Prize for Literature, noted that when a person receives a sting, it stays forever. One may learn to control it and keep it from driving him to revenge, but the sting remains. Always.

And yet, the love and happiness of the old neighborhood were dominant. The stings, when they came, helped to teach the lesson that Pete was not really so different from wolf-like humans. And bad people, like bad dogs, are also part of life.

Part II

The Immigrant Generation

Dad's parents died long before I was born, so the only grandparents I knew were Mom's parents, Marco and Sultana (Policar) Romey. Our family spent much time with them, and I often would sleep over at their house as a special treat.

Through them, my inner life was connected to their old country, Turkey.

Papoo Romey (Papoo is the word for grandfather among speakers of Judeo-Spanish) told of his childhood in Tekirdag. He described the synagogue there which was built right along the sea shore. The Jews of the town were poor, most of them merchants and peddlers. The Romey family worked in the kosher meat business.

"Why did you leave Tekirdag, Papoo? And why did you come all the way to Seattle?"

"Things were very difficult in Tekirdag. Poverty. Families were blessed with many children, but how were the children to be fed and clothed? Word reached us that a few Jews from our town had gone to America. They were making money. They had a better opportunity to advance themselves. Word came that a few Sephardic bachelors had gone to Seattle (See-aht-lee, as the Sephardim pronounced it) and found work in the fishing business. Also, Seattle looked like our part of Turkey—natural waters, abundant trees, mountains, open spaces. Some of our young people became restless. Why stay in Tekirdag where life was so hard, where there was hardly enough food for all of the children in the family? So some of us decided to go to America, to make money, to send back as much as we could to help our parents and families."

Nona Romey (Nona is the Judeo-Spanish word for grand-mother) had grown up in a small community on the Island of Marmara. She described one of the landmarks of that place, the casa del pasha, castle of the nobleman. Atop a high hill over-looking the city and the sea, a wealthy Turkish nobleman once decided to build a magnificent palace. He wanted it to be a spec-tacular testimony to his affluence and importance. The towns-people watched in wonder as the construction commenced and progressed. Apparently the nobleman fell on hard times and could not afford to complete the castle. It remained unfinished, an eternal monument to vanity and arrogance. People used to go to the unfinished castle with picnic lunches and would rejoice in its splendors. Here they were, simple poor people, having picnics in the Pasha's castle—while the pretentious Pasha himself was ruined.

Nona used to tell of the persecution of Jews which took place in Marmara, almost as a ritual. There were many Greek Christians who lived there. Generally, they got along well with the Jews. During the week before Easter, the Greeks would be told by their priests that the Jews were a cursed people who de-served punishment. The masses were inflamed with religious hatred. Nona told us that the Jews of Marmara would stay in their homes during the week of Easter. They boarded up their windows. Crowds of Greeks would beat any Jew they could find. They threw stones at the Jewish homes and stores. Nona never forgot the terror of hiding in her own house, as rocks pounded against the walls, as anti-Jewish taunts were shouted by the mob.

And then, after Easter, everything seemed to revert to "nor-mal." The Greeks greeted the Jews as old friends, as though nothing at all had happened.

The scars and fears remained in the hearts of the Jews. When the opportunity arose to leave Marmara and go to America, many of the young people were encouraged to emigrate.

Nona, then just a teenager, left her parents, knowing full well that she likely would never see them again. Indeed, she never did. Letters were sent back and forth, money was sent to the parents: but they never saw each other again.

"Why did you leave your parents if you knew you would not see them again?"

Nona would cry when she dealt with that question. "We had little choice. Our parents wanted us children to live in a better and safer place. They sacrificed everything for us. They themselves could not come, for many reasons. But they wanted us to have a chance for a better life."

I don't think Nona ever forgave herself for leaving her parents, even though they were the ones who encouraged her and her siblings to go to America. Psychologically and emotionally, Nona was deeply tied to the old country. In many ways, she never really left it.

Even as a youngster, I had a particular fascination with relatives who were born in the old country. They struck me as being people who had experienced great adventure, who were bold enough to take dangerous risks. Even though my grandparents and other relatives who were born in Turkey or Rhodes came to Seattle with little or no formal education, they were endowed with inner strength, courage and common sense. They were pioneers in a new world.

Papoo Romey was a man of sturdy faith. He was serious, but in a happy kind of way. He always seemed to have a Hershey bar in his pocket whenever his grandchildren turned up. He could be formal and dignified; but he could also be a genuine nonconformist. He often wore a seed-cap, with the brim turned over to one side. He could wear baggy pants and bright shirts and still appear to be proper and fashionable.

Before becoming a barber, he worked as a longshoreman. He used to walk back and forth to work, a distance of several miles, in order to save the bus fare. He barely managed to eke out a living to support his wife and children. On one summer day as he was walking home, the heat was so strong that he decided to step into a drugstore which had a soda fountain. He splurged and ordered himself a cold drink. He sat at the counter, tired and overheated, and slowly sipped the soda until he was rested and refreshed. He then put his hand into his pocket to take out some change to pay for the drink. To his mortification, he found that his pockets were absolutely empty. He sat at the counter, trying to figure out how he could get out of this situation without losing honor. Remarkably, a man sitting next to him was sensitive enough to recognize Papoo's predicament. He pulled a dime from his pocket and gave it to my grandfather—and then he left the store without even telling my grandfather who he was. Papoo paid for the soda and continued his walk back home. In recounting this amazing incident to his family, he concluded that the mystery man who had given him the dime was none other than Elijah the Prophet in disguise. Papoo offered prayers of thanks to the Almighty for sending Elijah to look after him and to spare him from shame. The moral: if a person is honest and works hard, the Almighty will find ways to help him.

Honor was an essential element in the life of the old country relatives. A sociologist who studied Sephardic immigrants in early 20th century America concluded that Sephardim saw themselves as a distinctive people with an inordinate pride bordering on stubbornness.

Papoo was a good example of this sociological observation. After working some years as a longshoreman, he decided to attend barber school so as to advance himself to a better job. He opened his barber shop in the Labor Temple located on 6th and University. Since many labor leaders and politicians frequented the Labor Temple, they often had their hair cut by my grandfather. Papoo was proud, for example, that he was the barber of Senator Warren Magnussen. But although he had a distinguished clientele, his income continued to be quite low.

In spite of his challenging economic condition and his lack of formal education, Papoo saw himself as being a nobleman. He held the popular tradition among Sephardic Jews that they descended from the aristocracy of Judea who had been exiled to Spain following the destruction of the ancient Temple in Jerusalem. To outsiders, he may have appeared to be just another semi-literate, financially strapped immigrant laborer. But he viewed himself as an aristocrat—even if temporarily reduced.

This powerful pride and sense of honor inspired the entire family. Papoo set the tone with majestic simplicity.

Papoo believed in things, he had principles. He did not apologize for his beliefs and policies, nor did he show hesitation in making decisions. He lived his life as though he were in control. In those days, the husband/father was the head of the household. He had to live up to the responsibilities of family leadership. Papoo did this with unabashed candor and confidence.

In raising his children, he had a number of old country rules of discipline. First, children had to respect their parents, like it or not. There was no talking back, no raising of voice, no protestations or arguments by the children. That was an axiom of family organization. The parents were in charge and knew what was best and what was right. The children had to remember their status: children!

When one child did something worthy of punishment, Papoo lined up all seven children and spanked them. He explained that all seven were guilty whenever any one of them did something wrong. They were responsible to look out for each other and see to it that everyone behaved. A lapse by one child meant that the other children had been derelict in their responsibility.

Papoo used to roll his own cigarettes. But it was clearly understood that the children, should not smoke. The boys would be allowed to smoke only after they had grown up and were on their own; the girls should never smoke.

The children (and later the grandchildren too) kissed Papoo's hand, after which he placed his hand on their head and gave them a blessing. When he entered a room, the family rose in respect and greeted him appropriately. Papoo structured family life in such a way that he was respected, even venerated, without needing to insist on his honor. He expected to be respected: and he was respected genuinely.

Papoo was a deeply religious man. He attended synagogue services regularly. He was president of the Sephardic Bikur Holim congregation in 1929; it was during his tenure that the congregation undertook to build its first building on 20th and Fir. During the 1930s, a newspaper known as "Progress" was published for the Sephardic community in Seattle. Papoo was featured in one of the issues as a pioneer Sephardic leader and activist.

Although his formal education was minimal, Papoo read and studied on his own. Each Friday night he would sit at a little table overlooking the yard and garden, have a glass of piping hot tea (with four teaspoons of sugar), and read the Torah portion of the week. On Sabbath afternoons, he regularly attended the Talmud class at the synagogue.

I often walked with Papoo from his house on 15th Avenue to the synagogue on 20th and Fir. There was a vacant lot on the way which had a narrow dirt path slashed across it in a diagonal. It was a short-cut. Instead of walking to the corner and then turning right, one could walk on the dirt path and save quite a few steps. Papoo never took the short-cut and never allowed me to do so. He insisted that we take derekh hamelekh, the king's road. Dignified and honorable people walk on proper paths, they do not cut through empty lots to save a little time and energy.

If Papoo conveyed strength and dignity, Nona conveyed these same qualities in a feminine way. She was virtually illiterate. She was afflicted with poor health for most of the years I knew her. Yet, she was idolized by the entire family as the role model of what a woman should and could be.

Nona was ingenious. She could create filling and tasty meals out of the simplest ingredients. Leftovers were converted into feasts. She was a gracious hostess.

Her grandchildren loved to spend time at her home. We always had fun. She had no toys in the house except for several worn out tennis balls. Yet, we were never bored. She played "question" games with us: she would say she was hiding in a color and we had to guess what she was thinking of. She would think of a person, or of an animal, vegetable or mineral—and we would ask her questions to discover the answer. She had a "Shabbat television." According to traditional Jewish law, it is forbidden to turn on electricity, including television, on Shabbat. So she had a hand operated viewmaster with a variety of slide programs. It was through this "Shabbat television" that I first saw Disneyland, and first experienced the sights of many of the cities of the world.

Nona taught us how to blow soap bubbles. We would go out to the back yard and pick a dandelion with as thick a stem as we could find. We cut the stem at both tips. Nona would mix some soap with water. We would use the stems like a straw, sucking in the soapy solution very gently. Sucking too hard resulted in a mouthful of soap, a bitter taste I still remember well. We would then blow softly until a bubble would form at the end of the stem. One needed to be patient and skillful to produce good, big bubbles; the joy of succeeding was one of the true joys of childhood. Other people bought soap bubbles and wands in the store, and their children could produce many more bubbles and with much less effort. But we felt sorry for them. They were missing all the fun.

We played games that required no toys or equipment: Mother May I, Hide and Seek, tag. With the old tennis balls, we spent hours playing Seven Up. With pebbles, we played: Guess Which Hand the Rock is in? We also played Steps. This was a game where the leader hid a pebble in one hand. The players sat on the first step. Each time a player guessed the correct hand that held the pebble, he or she advanced to the next step up. The first one to get to the top won.

When we went on a picnic on the shore of Lake Washington, Nona taught us how to go fishing. We would scour the beach until we could find a long enough stick to serve as a fishing pole. Nona then tied a piece of yarn to the stick and attached a safety pin at the bottom. For bait, she fastened pieces of cantaloupe rind on the safety pin. We fished for hours on end. We never caught anything. When we came back to the picnic table periodically to complain that we weren't catching any fish, Nona would change the bait and tell us to keep trying. Her laughter and joy at our fishing made us all happy.

Nona was a born story teller. She told about an elderly couple in Marmara, Dona and Levi, who were so romantic that they actually held hands in public. In a society that did not approve of public displays of affection, this was startling behavior. It was especially so since the couple were already old. Whenever Nona would see an older couple holding hands, she would say: "Dona con Levi," just like Dona and Levi of Marmara. Thus, this romantic couple of the old country became immortalized in this simple proverb.

She told stories about Joha. One of the heroes of Turkish folklore is Nassredin Hoja, a holy man who lived centuries ago. He was famous for his wit and his practical jokes. It is said that before he died, he instructed his heirs to erect a thick door in front of his gave. The door was to be fortified and locked so that no one could possibly break through it. But he also instructed that the door stand alone, without any walls, so that anyone could walk right past the door to the grave!

Since Nassredin Hoja was a Muslim religious figure, the Jews of the Ottoman Empire refashioned him into a Jewish person, inverting the title Hoja into the name Joha. Joha was associated with odd and humorous behavior. Inappropriate, awkward actions were known as echas de Joha, deeds of Joha. To deprecate someone's opinion, one simply said ya avlo Joha, it is Joha speaking.

Nona told Joha stories, some traditional and some that she improvised on her own. Here are a few examples.

One day, Joha's donkey ran away. He searched the entire city, asking everyone he saw: "Have you seen my donkey?" Each person answered "No. I have not seen your donkey." Joha then replied: "Blessed be the Lord." Someone finally asked Joha why he was blessing the Lord. Joha responded: "I bless the Lord that I was not on my donkey when he got lost. Otherwise I too would be lost now."

One day, Joha's neighbor asked to borrow his donkey. Joha replied: Unfortunately, my donkey has died." At that very moment, though, Joha's donkey brayed. The neighbor asked: "Why do you try to deceive me? I just heard your donkey's voice." Joha answered solemnly, as though deeply insulted. "What a skeptical person you are! You don't believe my voice, when here I am a man with a long white beard; and yet, you would believe the voice of a stupid donkey!"

Joha was walking down the street when he saw something sparkling in a garbage heap. He rushed over and picked it up. It was a mirror. Upon looking at it, Joha said: "What an ugly picture! No wonder its owner threw it into the garbage heap."

Joha's wife washed his pants and hung them on the clothesline outside to dry. The wind blew them off the line onto the ground. Joha exclaimed: "Praise the Lord that I was not wearing them at the time, otherwise I would have been hurt." He rushed to the synagogue to recite the blessing one recites upon having been saved from a possible disaster.

Here is an example of a story that describes Joha's wisdom. Three sages had heard that Joha was famous for his brilliant mind, so they decided to test him. The first sage asked: "Where is the center of the earth?" Joha answered calmly: "The center of the earth is exactly under the front left foot of my donkey." The sage asked how Joha could prove that. Joha answered: "All you have to do is measure the earth and then you will see that I am right."

The second sage then asked: "How many stars are there in the sky?" Joha answered: "There are as many stars as there are hairs on my donkey." When asked to prove this, Joha stated: "If you do not believe me, all you have to do is count them." The sage retorted: "But how can one count all the hairs on a donkey?"

Joha replied: "As easily as one can count all the stars in the sky."

Finally, the third sage tested Joha's wisdom. "How many hairs do I have in my beard?" he asked. Joha said: "You have as many hairs in your beard as my donkey has in its tail." When asked to prove this, Joha stated: "It is really very simple. Let us pluck the hairs from your beard and my donkey's tail, one at a time. In this way, we can count them easily."

All three sages recognized that Joha had defeated them. He indeed was the wisest of men.

My paternal grandfather, Bohor Yehudah Angel, died in 1925 when my father was only twelve years old. My father's mother, Bulissa Esther (Huniu) Angel, died in 1939, a year after my brother Bill was born. Their old country was the Island of Rhodes.

When they left Rhodes early in the 20th century, it was still under the governance of the Turks. For all practical purposes, the Judeo-Spanish civilization of the Jews of Rhodes was part of the mainstream Sephardic culture of the Jews of the Ottoman Empire. Yet, there were relatively minor differences that set the Jews of Rhodes apart—differences in pronunciation, in liturgical customs, and in folk traditions.

Where ever Jews of Rhodes migrated, they tended to stick together. Instead of blending in with other Sephardic communities, their first instinct was to establish their own self-help organizations and synagogues. This was true in Seattle, as in other cities. The Turkish Jews (my mother's family) were based at the Sephardic Bikur Holim synagogue; the Rhodes Jews (my father's family) were at the Congregation Ezra Bessaroth. In the old neighborhood, Bikur Holim was on 20th and Fir while Ezra Bessaroth was on 15th and Fir. Although only five blocks separated them, they functioned in many ways as though they were miles apart. Periodic discussions of merger always ended in failure.

Papoo Angel had a shoeshine stand in downtown Seattle. He was a hardworking, serious person, tall and strong. Because he had some religious education, he taught Hebrew to children in the Ezra Bessaroth religious school. He also served for a period as the synagogue's sexton. His income was small; his untimely death left my grandmother and her dependent children in financial difficulty. My father, although the youngest child, quickly understood that he also had to help provide income for his mother. He worked as a delivery boy for the morning newspaper; he sold boxes for people to sit on whenever there was a parade; after school, he worked in a variety of stores and fruit stands.

Nona Angel, in spite of her weak financial situation, was undaunted. She was a rotund woman with a determined, if somewhat jolly, expression on her face. She was actually a celebrity in the community, receiving visits from the great and small. Why? She was known to be able to perform cures. She could heal physical illnesses, emotional distress, psychological suffering. She even prescribed remedies for all sorts of personal problems. She had mastered the old-world folk wisdom; she knew which herbs to use and in what proportions. She was popularly known in the community as "La Gremma," her own way of pronouncing "the Grandma."

One of her major responsibilities was to help people ward off the evil eye. The belief in the evil eye goes back to antiquity. It was prevalent in the general society in Turkey and Rhodes, and was shared by the Sephardic Jews as well.

A person who was jealous of you or who wished you ill could cast an evil eye by looking at you in a malevolent way. Once a person had put an evil eye on you, you felt yourself under a wicked spell. Things would go wrong. Misfortune would follow misfortune.

People needed to protect themselves from incurring the evil eye. Preventive methods were best. First, people should avoid bragging or evoking envy. If they are praised for wealth, they should respond that they are actually deeply in debt, or that the wealth causes them grief; or they should praise God for His kindness. Wealthy people should be known for generosity to the poor and downtrodden.

Those complimented for their wisdom should play down this virtue by saying they are only using common sense and that so many others are far wiser than they. Indeed, one should never receive praise (or give praise) without saying Mashallah, as God wills. This word conveys humility and resignation, demonstrating that there is no intent to activate an evil eye.

Among believers in the evil eye, it is very bad manners to offer a direct compliment to anyone. I recall the story of a woman who praised a mother on her newborn baby: "what a homely child!" The mother responded with happiness and pride: "thank you, Mashallah."

La Gremma used folkloric methods for warding off the evil eye. Blue beads were effective. A necklace or bracelet of blue beads interspersed with whole cloves was even better. Garlic was especially efficacious. For example, one should always keep a few cloves of garlic in a kitchen drawer and in the glove compartment of one's car. Rutha (rue) was also a proven success against the evil eye. By keeping a sprig of rutha in your pocket or putting it behind your ear, you were defending yourself against the forces of the evil eye.

If a person was already afflicted by the evil eye, then a cure was needed. La Gremma used a traditional method known as enseredura, isolation. Toward the end of a lunar month, the patient was locked alone in a room. Soon after midnight, La Gremma would ask the person to name the one who had cast the evil eye on him or her. Upon receiving this information, she would go to the home of the named person, wash the steps to the house, collect the water from this washing, and bring it back to the patient. She would make the patient drink some, while she recited various phrases and incantations. The result: the person would be cured and would leave La Gremma, thanking her for breaking the wicked spell. La Gremma would beam with joy.

Another method for removing the evil eye also entailed isolation of the patient. At sundown of the first day of isolation, La Gremma gave the patient a concoction made of sweet marjoram, orange blossoms and sugar. This was given again at midnight and at noon of the next day. She also sprinkled some powder on the patient. On the third day, she gave some mocha to drink and then led the patient to a hot bath. The patient was smeared with a cleansing solution, as La Gremma recited the necessary formulae. After the bath, the patient was cured.

My father, who helped his mother in effecting these cures, told me that his mother was remarkably successful. She brought cheer and mental relief to depressed and anxiety-ridden men and women. "She knew her cures alright," Dad said, "but mainly she was a masterly psychologist. She understood peoples' needs, their fears and sorrows. She knew exactly what to do to restore them to health and happiness."

Dad told of the time when one of the young men of the family was about to announce his engagement to a non-Jewish woman. La Gremma was horrified at the idea of a family member marrying out of the faith. She came up with a solution.

First, she found out the name and address of the prospective bride. Then, she made my father go to a store and buy a quantity of lard. At midnight, she had my father—then a teenager—take the lard to the address of the young woman in question. La Gremma instructed him to smear the lard on the steps and porch of the bride's house and then return home immediately. Dad always recalled this incident with some terror, remembering how frightened he was that he would be caught for trespassing and damaging property.

Dad followed La Gremma's instructions even though he thought the whole enterprise was outrageous. But it worked. Within a few days the engagement was broken off. Shortly afterward, the young man became engaged to a Jewish young lady. When they were married, La Gremma beamed with joy that perhaps no one but my father could have fully understood.

Although my grandparents Angel both died before I was born, they have had a strong influence on me. When I chose a topic for my doctoral dissertation at Yeshiva University, it was "The History of the Jews of the Island of Rhodes." This project went on to become my first published book. It was a topic that had been aching within me. In studying the history of the Jews of Rhodes, I was trying to come closer to the world of my own grandparents.

In the summer of 1974, I travelled to Rhodes to complete my doctoral research.

A grandchild visiting the city of his dead grandparents for the first time searches for hidden messages in every street sign and store front. Each winding road whispers secrets that cannot be easily deciphered and memories that can no longer be remembered.

The Jewish community of Rhodes had come to a virtual end on July 24, 1944—a year and one day before my birth. On that day, the Nazis deported the nearly 2000 Jews still living in Rhodes. Very few survived the Nazi death camps. The Sephardic community of Rhodes began as a result of the expulsion of Jews from Spain in 1492. It ended in the ashes of Nazi concentration camps.

During the ten days I spent in Rhodes, I tried to recreate in my mind the Jewish community as it had been when my grandparents had lived there. I wandered through the winding streets of the former Jewish Quarter within the old walled city of Rhodes. I found a few Hebrew inscriptions on some buildings. I located the sites of now destroyed synagogues, as well as the one synagogue that still stands. Only a gate of the Alliance Israelite Universelle school survived the bombings of World War II; the school itself was demolished.

I walked along the Mandraki and observed the bustle and

commotion of the merchants on one side, and the eternal sea on the other side. Out in the distance were los tres molinos, the three windmills dating back to medieval times when the Knights of St. John ruled the island.

The Jewish Quarter was filled with tourists. The main square, that the Jews had called la calle ancha, the broad street, was lined with tourist shops and eateries. The main street in the former Jewish Quarter was renamed after the war: it is called the Street of the Hebrew Martyrs. Except for the street sign and a few other clues that Jews had once lived here, the Jewish presence has been almost entirely wiped out. The homes that Jews had once occupied are now filled with Greek families. The stores that Jews had once owned now cater to tourists. I had the feeling of being at a carnival that had been erected on a cemetery.

On Friday night, I stood at the reader's desk in the Kahal Shalom, the remaining synagogue in the once thriving Jewish Quarter. I conducted the Sabbath services according to the style of the Rhodes Jews, as I had learned it growing up in Seattle among Jews of Rhodes origin. I imagined that my grandparents had prayed in this same synagogue when it had been crowded and alive; they had sung the same melodies, uttered the same words. That Friday night all but four people at the service were tourists. Some of us were of Rhodes descent, searching for shadows and sparks from our past, thinking we had found something but unsure of what it was.

After services, I walked alone through the old Juderia. Although it was bustling with activity, as far as the Jews are concerned it is mainly filled with memories of death.

A plaque is affixed to the synagogue. It lists the family names of the Jews who had been murdered by the Nazis. My eyes immediately, spontaneously, found the name Angel—relatives I had never known, who had been deported to their deaths one year and one day before I was born. This was as close as I had come to meeting Uncle Joseph, his wife Sinyoru, and his four children—my cousins—Leon, Bulissa, Jacob and Sarah.

My grandparents were among the lucky ones to have left

Rhodes in the early 20th century. Even though they died before I was born, they helped create a living memory that they transmitted to the future generations of their family.

Whenever I return to Seattle, I drive through the old neighborhood in the central district. I go to the houses that contain my childhood.

The psychiatrist and philosopher, Viktor Frankl, has noted that the truest and surest aspects of life are in the past. They have already been lived; they are done and can never be changed. While the future is uncertain, the past is fixed. The older one grows, the more of life has been deposited in the secure treasury of history. Looking back, one sees what has been done and accomplished; looking ahead, one can only hope and pray. Being an elder, then, has its genuine virtues and pleasures.

And yet, when one contemplates the past through the prism of memory, the result is not necessarily to find certainty. Rather, memory tends to focus on some things and ignore others. Memory makes some people glow in a halo of greatness, while others are remembered with their many defects. What we remember is not an exact description of the past; it is, for all sorts of reasons, that which made the deepest and most lasting impressions on us. We incorporate those memories into our own lives; the remembered past lives on within us.

When I go through the old neighborhood, I sometimes feel that I am once again a little boy who belongs there. But then I shake my head and realize that I am only a stranger to the people who now fill the houses and the neighborhood.

On a summer day many years ago, my wife Gilda and I drove to my childhood home at 511 28th Avenue. Listening to me reminisce, Gilda asked me if we could knock on the door of the house and find out if the owner would let us take a quick look through. I told her that I did not want to do that. She hesitated for a moment and then got out of the car. She went up the front steps of the house and knocked on the door.

A jovial African-American woman appeared at the entrance. My wife told her that I had grown up in this house. Could we take a quick look at it and perhaps snap a few photographs? The owner smiled and told Gilda that this would be fine with her. Gilda waved to me to come upstairs. I came out of the car but said I didn't really want to bother anyone, that I was happy just to see the house from the outside.

Gilda thanked the owner of the house and then came back down the steps of the front porch. She took a few pictures of the house from the front and then went up the long driveway to the back of the house where she took several more photographs in the backyard.

When she returned to the car, she put the camera in her purse and looked at me in wonderment. As we drove off, I told her about the backyard of the house…the old tree I used to climb, the little patch of dirt where we used to grow parsley and mint, the white picket fence that separated us from our neighbor's dog, Pete.

"Why didn't you go look at the back yard again now that you had the opportunity? And why didn't you go into the house when the lady said we could take a look around?"

"I guess I would rather leave the past in my mind the way I remember it. This house is not the thing I want; it's the house in my mind that I want to keep."

When Gilda had the roll of film developed, we found that only one of her photographs of the old house had been developed successfully. The only picture that came out was a shot of the outside front of the house, the house as we saw it from the car, the house as I wanted to keep it in my memory.

On our visits to Seattle, we not only would visit the old neighborhood. We also would visit the Sephardic cemetery. My mother and father are buried side by side. Mom had died in 1983, and Dad passed away in 1991. Walking through the cemetery, we would visit the graves of my parents, grandparents, uncles and aunts, and so many relatives and friends.

For me, a visit to the Sephardic cemetery of Seattle proves the wisdom of the ancient Jewish sages who referred to a cemetery as beth hahayyim, the home of the living. Though this term is a euphemism, it also is--in a significant sense—true. Those who are laid to rest in the cemetery have indeed died; yet, their lives continue to influence those who loved and knew them. They have died; but their memories live on, at least for the next generation or two.

The rows of neatly-kept tombstones remind me of many lives, many stories. Part of my own life is safely deposited in this beth hahayyim.

Bits and pieces of lives, bits and pieces of memories.

Not far from the grave of my Nona Romey is the grave of Uncle Moshe, my father's oldest brother. Uncle Moshe and his wife, Aunty Bohora, lived just around the block from our house. Their red brick home was on the corner of Jefferson and Temple Place (later to be called Empire Way, and now Martin Luther King Jr. Way).

Uncle Moshe spoke in a loud voice. Everything about him conveyed strength and determination. My Uncle Avner told us that Uncle Moshe had to flee from Rhodes to America early in the 20th century. When he had been a worker in a bakery in Rhodes, someone had come into the store and had made some nasty comments to him. Uncle Moshe lifted a large iron pan and smashed the man's head open. No one could insult him and get away with it!

When his parents learned what their first-born son had done, they quickly arranged for him to leave for Seattle, where several Rhodes Jews had already settled.

Whether or not this story is actually true, it left a special aura on the character of Uncle Moshe. We all knew that it could have been true. We all learned reverence for him; no one wanted to raise his ire.

He was loud, energetic and tough. He took chances. He feared no one.

Uncle Moshe used to call me by a series of nicknames: Marconi, Macaroni, Markooch, Markoocho. Even in his toughness, he could be soft and gentle. When I remember him, I envision him with a wan smile on his face. But his advice to me was consistent: don't let anyone push you around; don't be afraid to take risks; stand up for your rights.

In the mid-1950s, the city planners decided to widen Temple Place in order to create Empire Way, a much larger road that could handle a lot more traffic. A problem arose, though, when it became clear that the road would cut right through Uncle Moshe's house.

The city officials approached Uncle Moshe and informed him of the plans. They offered to buy his house at an attractive price.

"What will you do to my house if you buy it?" Uncle asked.

"We will demolish it so that the highway can run through the lot."

"It's not for sale," said Uncle Moshe defiantly.

No amount of persuasion or financial incentives could budge him. It was his house, he liked it, no one could tell him what to do. He was not about to sell his home only to have it destroyed. Certain things in life were worth fighting for, and one's own home was one of them.

Dad tried to point out the advantages of selling the house. "Listen, Moshe, this is a great opportunity for you. You can make a nice profit and buy a new house, a better one. In any case, you can't win this time. The city will build its highway whether you like it or not."

"You don't understand," explained Uncle Moshe. "This is

America, not a tyranny. In America people are free, we have rights. We can't let ourselves be thrown out of our own house. The government will defend my rights."

The planners were able to settle with all other home owners whose property would be affected by the construction of Empire Way. Uncle Moshe was the last holdout.

Finally, one of the city officials came up with an idea and made a suggestion to Uncle Moshe. "The city will not buy your house and will not demolish it. Instead, the city will move your house a few yards back so that it will be out of the way of the highway. It will pay you for the land it expropriates as well as for the inconvenience to you and your family."

Uncle Moshe was exuberant. "Who said I couldn't beat City Hall?" he gloated.

And so it was. A construction company came, picked up the house on huge beams, and moved it out of the path of the new road. Uncle Moshe had won.

The victory was short lived. The house was moved only a few yards back, but somehow that changed everything. Uncle Moshe felt that the house had been damaged in the moving process. As he looked out his window at the construction of the highway, he began to realize that the world outside his house was changing. More people, more cars, more noise, more air pollution. In the end, he had wanted to live in his home as it had been, on the quiet corner of Jefferson and Temple Place. Now there was to be a steady stream of traffic on the highway that ran right by his house.

It was not too long before Uncle Moshe died.

The first funeral I attended was the funeral of Uncle Moshe. I was eleven or twelve years old. We went into the Jewish chapel on twelfth and Alder. A large gathering of family and friends had come to pay their final respects.

I saw the casket in front of the room but did not know what it was. I asked Dad what was in the box. "Uncle Moshe is in there," he answered simply.

I remember my perplexity. "How did Uncle Moshe let anyone

put him in a box?"

"He can't fight anymore," Dad said somberly.

That is when I first started to understand what death was.

If Uncle Moshe was loud, his younger brother Ralph was every bit his equal. When Uncle Moshe and Uncle Ralph were together, the volume of their conversations was truly awesome. As a newly-wed, Mom had been terrified to have these brothers-in-law in her home. Dad reassured her that they were both good men, but they tended to speak in loud voices. Mom never entirely lost her fear of Uncle Moshe and Uncle Ralph.

Uncle Ralph's wife, Aunty Hanulah, was a really lovely, sweet woman, with a ready smile on her face. She and Mom had a warm relationship. So as long as Aunty Hanulah was with Uncle Ralph, Mom was not nervous.

After the death of Uncle Moshe, Uncle Ralph's voice became softer, his manner somewhat more reserved. He, too, was getting old. His eldest brother had died; he saw himself as being next in line.

One day—after we had already moved to the new neighborhood in Seward Park—Uncle Ralph (who was still living in the old neighborhood) telephoned my father. He was planning to attend synagogue services the next morning at the new Ezra Bessaroth building. He told Dad that he wanted to come to our home for breakfast after services. Being a request from an elder brother, Dad was obliged to comply. This situation was mainly of concern to Mom. After all, Dad left for work early in the morning and he would not be home for breakfast with Uncle Ralph.

Mom prepared a breakfast of hard boiled eggs, sliced tomatoes, sweet rolls, homemade white cheese swimming in oil, and raki (a strong anise-flavored alcoholic beverage favored by Turkish and Greek people). I was surprised by this menu. How could anyone eat this kind of food so early in the morning? What was wrong with toast, cereal and a cup of coffee? Mom smiled. "Uncle Ralph will like this much better."

And so it was. He arrived at our home and ate his breakfast as though it was the most normal morning meal in the world; and he drank several shots of raki without blinking an eye. After he had eaten to his satisfaction, Mom told him politely that she had to get to her household chores. Uncle Ralph was unperturbed. He had travelled all the way to the Seward Park neighborhood and he wanted to stay longer. He said that he would be quite content to sit in the dining room near the window that overlooked the street. He sat there for several hours, quietly, meditatively. He didn't yell, didn't raise his voice, didn't make any demands. He just sat gazing at the passing cars, lost in his thoughts. He had changed; perhaps he was preparing himself for his forthcoming death.

I tried to make small talk with Uncle Ralph. He nodded politely but kept his eyes focused out the window. "So many cars," he said softly. "So many cars. Where are they coming from? Where are they going? Why is everyone in such a rush?" He nodded his head slowly and sipped raki. "It is time for quiet and rest. Too much traffic, too much noise. What does it all mean and where does it get you?"

Several months after his breakfast at our house, Uncle Ralph died. He was buried in the Sephardic cemetery in a grave adjoining that of Papoo Romey who had died a week earlier. They were buried in a new row of graves against the back fence of the cemetery.

And just beyond the fence was the highway, cars rushing by in an endless procession.

Uncle Avner was caught in the middle. His two older brothers, Moshe and Ralph, demanded his obedient loyalty; and he gave it to them. It was his duty to respect his older brothers and he would do so even to his own detriment.

But his two younger brothers, Ray and Victor (my father), made their own way in life. While respectful of their older brothers, Ray and Victor were part of the new Americanized generation. They strove for independence. Ray and Victor started their own businesses, and Avner found himself—more than once—working for his younger brothers. For Uncle Avner, this seemed to be an inversion of the normal order of things. He should have been the boss, not the employee.

Uncle Avner, the middle son of the family, was consumed with his need to be honored and respected. He was stubborn, hot tempered and demanding. He felt that no one adequately appreciated him; so he often reminded people of their obligation to honor him. This tactic only served to exacerbate his problem; the more honor he demanded, the less he received.

One of my early memories of Uncle Avner was an incident that occurred on a Sabbath morning in the old Ezra Bessaroth synagogue building on 15th and Fir. Following services, there was a memorial service for a deceased parent of one of the members. It was customary on such occasions for families to provide refreshments in the vestry room adjoining the sanctuary. The usual fare included sweet rolls, hard boiled eggs, Greek olives, raisins, pickles, sliced tomatoes, whiskey and raki. On this particular Sabbath, the family provided the refreshments—but not enough to go around. By the time Uncle Avner got to the table, there were no more hard boiled eggs. His face flushed, Uncle Avner loudly demanded a hard boiled egg. He was told that there were none left. This infuriated him. He started to shout: "Why don't I get an egg? Am I not important enough? Do only bigshots get eggs? Why is the family so cheap that they can't provide enough eggs for all the members? I'm entitled to an egg just like everyone else." Dad tried to calm his brother down but it was no use. Uncle Avner kept on shouting until people edged their way out of the room; soon, there was no one left to listen to his grievances. I clung to my father in terror. He told me: "Don't be afraid. Uncle Avner has a bad temper. In truth, he is right. There should have been enough eggs for everyone. But once he lost his temper, he lost his argument. Once he started to shout, he was wrong."

That event was typical of Uncle Avner's attitude. No one could slight his feelings without hearing about it from him. At a buffet reception, Mom once made the mistake of inviting Uncle Avner to the table to help himself to some food. He raged at her: "What do you mean by that? I don't go to any table for food! My wife serves me my food! I don't stand on line for anyone." At a memorial service, the reader asked Uncle Avner to be quiet so that services could begin. Uncle Avner responded in a fury: "No one tells me to be quiet! I tell others when to be quiet!" He kept on talking for a few minutes until he had proved his point. Only after he was ready did the service begin.

If Uncle Avner was ornery and willful, his wife—Aunty Suzie—was his equal. She did not put up with his outbursts. She kept him in line, and together they raised a really fine group of children.

Uncle Avner's quest for respect got him nowhere. His older brothers looked down on him as a younger brother. His younger brothers did not have patience to constantly appease him. His wife was not subservient to him. His relatives and the community at large did not appreciate his temper tantrums.

Yet Uncle Avner had his virtues. He was genuinely loyal and straightforward. He was devoted to Rabbi Isidore Kahan, rabbi of Ezra Bessaroth, and often drove Rabbi Kahan where ever he needed to go.

As he grew older, Uncle Avner mellowed somewhat. He and Aunty Suzie became active in the Golden Age Club sponsored by the Jewish Community Center. They helped out at the Kline Galland Home for the Aged. Uncle Avner, now an old man, apparently gave up his lifelong quest for honor. It didn't matter much anymore if people gave him the respect he thought he deserved or if they ignored. Him. He would just do what he liked, try to get along, help others to enjoy their golden years.

Amazingly enough, in his last years, he actually became well liked and respected. As soon as he had given up his life's battle for respect, that is when he started to win respect. Only when he admitted his own defeat did he achieve victory.

Aunty Victoria made us laugh.

She was my father's eldest sister. I never knew her husband. Whenever I asked about him, my parents became very serious and said he was at Sedro-Woolley. It took me a while before I dared to ask what Sedro-Woolly was.

I eventually learned that Sedro-Woolley is a town in upstate Washington, the location of a mental institution. Aunty Victoria's husband had been hurt in a serious automobile accident, leaving him with permanent injury to his brain.

In her husband's absence, Aunty Victoria had to raise her family. Being poor did not make things any easier. She worked hard. In spite of her many problems, she was optimistic and full of fun. Although she was highly intelligent, her playful spirit led her sometimes to play the role of a scatterbrain. She enjoyed leading people on, teasing them a bit.

Aunty Victoria had her own way of understanding things. Mom once told her of a telephone call she had received from a distant relative in South Africa. The relative was a young lady whose grandparents had emigrated from Rhodes to Rhodesia (now Zimbabwe). The family later moved to Capetown. She called my mother to ask if she could stay at our home during a projected visit to Seattle. The problem was that she intended this visit to last for six months to a year. Mom politely declined.

Aunty Victoria was intrigued with this story. "And how old is she?" she asked.

"About nineteen or twenty."

"1920? If she was born in 1920, she's already well on in years. Why isn't she married?"

"No, Victoria," Mom explained, "I said she is nineteen or twenty years old."

"Es wad I say, (That's what I said)," Aunty Victoria insisted. "If she was born in 1920, she should already be married."

After several more attempts to clarify the facts, Mom gave up. "You're right, Victoria. If she calls again, I'll tell her that she should have already gotten married since she was born in 1920."

"Es wad I say," nodded Aunty Victoria with a big smile, proud of her victory.

When Mom was in the hospital for the birth of my brother David, Aunty Victoria moved into our house to help keep things in order. Each morning she would come into the kitchen as though in a daze. She would say nothing, respond to no greeting or question. She went to the refrigerator, poured herself a glass of orange juice, puckered up her face, opened her eyes wide and then sang out: Good morning! For Aunty Victoria, the day did not start until she had her orange juice.

But then, she shook off her languor and became a knot of energy. She cleaned, cooked, rushed around. She sent my father to work after having packed him a huge lunch. She dressed up the children. She never negotiated with us: just instructed us.

One of the severest trials of her stay in our house was bath time. It was her considered opinion that the hot water from the tap was not really hot. A real bath required heating a pot of water on the stove and then pouring it into the tub—when we were in the tub! We dreaded taking baths. We pleaded with her, begged her. It made no difference. To bathe properly required hot water; only hot water can make one clean; and hot water is obtained by heating it on the stove. That's it. Period.

When we later complained to Mom about these scalding baths, she said: "Well, at least you know you got clean and killed all the germs." Aunty Victoria was vindicated.

Whenever she heard a car honking outside, Aunty Victoria

would get up and call out, "I comee (I'm coming)." I once asked her why she did that., "Well, maybe the car is coming to pick me up to take me someplace."

"But Aunty, people honk the horns of their cars all the time. They aren't coming here to pick you up."

"But how do you know? Can you be so sure? Maybe this time it is someone coming for me."

"But you know the truth, Aunty."

"I do know the truth, little Markito, but you don't know the truth." And that is where the conversation ended. I never raised the question again. Nor did anyone else.

Aunty Victoria often called me cusuegroo, in-law, in the Rhodes pronunciation of Judeo-Spanish. Of course, I was her nephew not her in-law. Aunty Victoria followed her own logic. I was named after my mother's father. My grandfather was an in-law to the Angel family. By simple transference, I (who carried my grandfather's name) became a personification of my grand-father.

She was consistent in this practice. She called my sister, Bernice "Mommy," since Bernice was named after Bulissa Es-ther, mother of Aunty Victoria. She once scolded a young child for not having greeted her respectfully enough. He was named after his grandfather who owned a grocery store that Aunty Vic-toria patronized. She told the bewildered child: "Bension, why don't you treat me better? After all, I am a good customer. I pay my bills. I never give your trouble." The child had no idea what was going on; but the rest of us had a good laugh.

In following her own rule of conservation of characters, those who shared the same name became, in some special sense, one person. The grandparents and grandchildren, linked together by their names, became identical in Aunty Victoria's playful version of reality. We laughed at this quirk of hers; but in her humorous way, she was articulating a very profound understanding of the nature of a family, of the mystery of the generations.

Aunty Victoria, through her understanding of the role of names, was apt to integrate new acquaintances into her world-view by making their names more familiar to her. In so doing, she changed a person from being a stranger to being a long-time friend. When I came to Seattle for Passover in 1967 with my wife-to-be Gilda, Aunty Victoria was quick to change Gilda's name to Zimbul, a popular name among Sephardic women from Turkey.

"No," my mother explained. "Her name is Gilda, not Zimbul."

Aunty's eyes squinted a bit; her brain seemed to be processing this information. "Es wad I say, Zimbul." She gave Gilda a warm hug. Gilda became Zimbul and was happy to go along with her new name. Gilda, who was 100% Ashkenazic, liked the idea of having a Sephardic name. So everyone was happy.

Aunty Victoria was a patriotic American. She decided to become a citizen. She learned to read English. She studied the various facts that one must know in order to pass the citizenship test. When the day of the test came, we all wished her well…but never expected that she would pass.

"Don't worry," she assured us. "I will pass. I love America."

After the test, she gleefully gave us a report. She had indeed passed.

"They asked me questions and I gave them answers. I kept telling them how much I love America. I am not sure if I understood them or if they understood me. Finally, they asked me the name of the President of the United States. I told them I was proud to be in America, in a free country, where a Jew can be President. Our President is Isaac Hower. We call him Ike." (For Aunty Victoria, the names Isaac and Ike were exclusively Jewish names!)

"But Aunty," I protested, "the President's name is Eisenhower."

"Es wad I say, Isaac Hower."

"No, it's Eisenhower. Dwight David Eisenhower."

"Es wad I say, Isaac Hower. God bless him."

I looked at Aunty Victoria's face and she was red with suppressed laughter.

"You're right, Aunty. You're always right."

"Es wad I say."

In her old age, Aunty Victoria never lost her sense of humor. But her face was serious more often, and her laughing eyes started to show glints of sadness, tiredness. She had lived long enough to see one husband die at a young age, one husband institutionalized, some of her children and grandchildren marry out of the faith. She was traumatized when she had to move from the old neighborhood in the central district to the new neighborhood in Seward Park. She had lived in the old neighborhood for over fifty years and was at home there.

One Saturday night, our family went to visit Aunty Victoria. We found her sitting on her front porch staring into the dark, cloudy sky. The lights of her house were off.

"Buenas semanas," we called to her with the traditional greeting at the conclusion of the Sabbath on Saturday night.

Aunty Victoria waved her hands. "No, Shabbat is not over. I don't see three stars yet." (According to tradition, the Sabbath is deemed to have ended once it is night. Seeing three stars is an indication that it is truly night and that the Sabbath has concluded.)

"But, Victoria," Dad responded with a smile, "it's very cloudy tonight. Of course you can't see three stars. Sunset was long ago! Shabbat is over."

"No," said Aunty Victoria adamantly. "If I don't see three stars, Shabbat is not over. I am going to wait here until Shabbat ends."

"Don't be silly," Dad prodded. "You will be staying on the porch all night. It's too cloudy to see stars tonight."

Aunty Victoria did not budge. We stayed with her for an hour or so, but she would not concede that Shabbat was over. On the way home, Dad was in a somber mood. "Aunty Victoria doesn't want Shabbat to be over. She doesn't want anything to change. She knows that Shabbat is over and she knows that everything is changing."

I don't know how late she sat on her porch waiting to see three stars.

Uncle Marco and Aunty Luna were an interesting pair. Uncle Marco was a perpetual joker. He loved a good time, loved to laugh. Aunty Luna, my father's sister, was serious and devout. Uncle Marco enjoyed smoking cigars and playing pinochle; Aunty Luna found happiness in prayer and religious devotion. Uncle Marco didn't mind cutting corners; Aunty Luna was a stickler for detail.

They had unusual quarrels. Uncle Marco was once recounting a car trip they took to California. He indicated that he got a speeding ticket in San Francisco. "No," said Aunty Luna solemnly, "we got the ticket near Sacramento." Uncle Marco strenuously maintained that the ticket was received in San Francisco. Aunty Luna was adamant that it was received near Sacramento. The disagreement continued for the better part of an hour, until another relative arrived who had been in the car with them. "Now," said Uncle Marco with glee, "now we have an eye witness. Tell us: where did we receive the speeding ticket?" The witness answered promptly: "Just outside Los Angeles." And of course this generated a three way controversy that went on for another half hour.

"What difference does it make where you got the ticket?" Mom asked innocently.

Then all three combatants shouted my mother down. "What do you mean what difference does it make? Aren't you interested in truth? Isn't it important to establish fact from falsehood?"

As things turned out, Aunty Luna was correct; she usually was. Uncle Marco was forced to admit it. "So who cares where I got the ticket? Why make such a big deal over a trifling detail?" Then he laughed and lit up a cigar.

One time they quarreled about the year of Aunty Luna's birth. Aunty maintained that she was born in 1899. Uncle argued vehemently that she was actually born in 1898.

Aunty: "Don't you think I should know the year I was born?"

Uncle: "You know, but you just don't want to admit the truth."

Aunty: "What are you talking about?"

Uncle: "You just want everyone to think you're a spring chicken, younger than you actually are."

Aunty: "Are you serious?"

Uncle: Laughter.

Uncle Marco told us stories of his childhood in Rhodes. As a teenager, he had been nicknamed palyachi because he was an acrobat. He could do somersaults and handstands; he could juggle; he could outrun his friends. He was known for his sense of humor and for his love of pranks.

He told us that ships bringing merchandise to Rhodes would anchor in the deep water off shore. Workers from Rhodes would row boats to the ships, transfer the merchandise into the boats, and row back to shore.

Some ships brought cargoes of food items, including lemons. Uncle Marco used to swim the long distance to the ship, sneak himself aboard, snatch a sack of lemons, and then swim back to shore with his loot. He would then show off his booty to all the young men and women he happened to meet in the street.

Uncle Marco recounted these exploits with great enthusiasm and joy. "Why would you want to steal lemons?" I asked him. "And why would you brag about stealing them?"

Uncle Marco's face broke into a broad, happy grin. "Hey, I was palyachi, I was a great swimmer, a great athlete. I was faster than anyone. I could snatch lemons right from under their noses and swim away without them catching me. It wasn't lemons I wanted. It was the recognition."

"But what did you prove?"

"Everyone knew that we Jews were smart. Everyone knew that we were good workers. But they used to think that we were weak and cowardly. So I showed them: we are not only smart and industrious; we are also brave and strong. We could beat them at their own game. They had to respect us. My lemons were a badge of honor."

"Are you still proud of what you did?"

Uncle Marco laughed. "Everyone has to do something daring in life. Everyone has to make a statement. It was a great thing to be palyachi. It was a great thing to prove that a Jew could be strong, quick and brave. They never forgot, believe me, they never forgot."

My grandfather Angel's brother, Yosef, was reverentially known as Hermano Yosef or Tio Yosef (brother Yosef or Uncle Yosef). These were terms of respect that Sephardim used for elders, even when they were not actually related to them.

By the time I was born, he was already an old man. Tio Yosef had a light complexion; his hair was white as snow. His head nodded ceaselessly, as though he were constantly saying "no, no, no." I never heard him raise his voice. He was the epitome of gentleness and piety. Tio Yosef enjoyed the respect of our family and the community at large.

His son and daughter-in-law, in whose home he lived, were first cousins. Most of their children were born with physical or mental handicaps. The household in which they lived was not an easy one. Money was scarce; problems were abundant. With all the difficulties, though, Tio Yosef remained a model of calmness and holiness. "All is for the best," he would say. "Praise the Lord for He is good, His mercy endures forever."

Although he was elderly and frail, Tio Yosef found the strength and energy to go to the synagogue often. After the daily prayers had been concluded, he stayed in the synagogue to repair old prayer books and tattered prayer shawls. He made sure that the synagogue was kept neat and clean.

Tio Yosef also cared deeply about the community's cemetery.

He thought that a society could be judged by the way it treated its dead. A properly maintained cemetery showed that the community cared about its departed relatives and friends. It demonstrated that love and respect transcend death.

During the mid-1950s, the Sephardic community of Seattle was in need of new land for a cemetery. The old cemetery was almost filled with graves. Each new death brought sadness not only to the deceased's family, but to the entire community: the cemetery now had one less space for a new grave.

The leaders of the community recognized and acknowledged the problem. Committees were formed, suggestions were made—but little was done. A new cemetery entailed a large expenditure of funds for the land, for a chapel, for maintenance. One of the Sephardic congregations, Ezra Bessaroth, was raising funds in order to build a new sanctuary in the Seward Park district. The other Sephardic congregation, Bikur Holim, was coming to the realization that it too would have to move to Seward Park-- and to raise the money needed for that eventuality. In sum, the community was facing huge expenditures. How would Seattle's Sephardim also be able to pay for a new cemetery?

If the community could not wait long to make its plans, the cemetery also could not wait. People died. They needed to be buried. Families could not be told that a new cemetery would be available some years from now, whenever the money could be raised. There was no negotiating with a dead body.

As community leaders struggled with this dilemma, Tio Yosef decided that he personally would take responsibility for raising the funds for the cemetery. He saw this project as his last mitzvah, a final meritorious deed of pious devotion before he himself would die. Caring for the dead is considered an especially great act of piety since it is done with pure idealism, without expectation of reward. The dead cannot say thank you.

Once he adopted this project, Tio Yosef was infused with newfound energy. He was tireless in his solicitation of funds. "A good name is better than precious oil," he would say. "Contribute generously so that you will share in this great mitzvah."

He went to businesses and homes. He solicited funds from the grocers and fish dealers; from the shoemakers and storekeepers. He solicited from the rich and from the poor. He would not be put off or rejected. "The honor of our community is at stake. We must care for our dead with love and reverence."

Tio Yosef could often be seen walking throughout the neighborhood in search of donations. His head nodded "no, no, no;" but his intensity was "yes, yes, yes." He used his cane as an extra leg, giving him more strength. People marveled at his devotion.

Tio Yosef contributed generously from his own meek assets. "I cannot ask others to do what I won't do myself," he explained. "I am ready to sacrifice. Let everyone else do the same."

I remember my parents discussing the incredible selflessness of Tio Yosef. He had a fire within him. He wanted to accomplish his goal as quickly as possible. He could not be repressed.

At last, the goal was achieved. Enough money was raised to buy the land and build a chapel. Tio Yosef beamed with pride and joy. The cemetery and the chapel were very much his victory. He not only collected funds but inspired others to donate.

The day arrived when the cemetery and chapel were to be dedicated. A large crowd gathered, and Tio Yosef was congratulated and thanked by many. In a special way, this was his day. He had completed his last mitzvah with admirable results.

At the dedication ceremony, it was announced that the chapel would be dedicated in the name of a wealthy couple who had contributed a handsome amount to the cemetery project. The speaker offered profuse praise of this philanthropic couple.

My father was disappointed by the committee's decision. It was Tio Yosef who had rallied the community to support the project. He had given his time and effort; he had contributed of his own meager funds with amazing generosity. The poor make the greatest sacrifices, but the rich are given the honor.

My mother nodded with calm wisdom: "No one said that life is fair."

In the days ahead, Tio Yosef retained his pious demeanor. He showed no frustration, anger or bitterness. Perhaps his head nodded "no, no, no" with a bit more sadness.

"Everything is for the best," he said. "Praise the Lord for He is good, His mercy endures forever."

Uncle Ralph Policar, my Nona's older brother, was the first of his siblings to leave Marmara for Seattle. He arrived in 1906 at the age of 18. He first earned money shining shoes, and later went to work in the fish business, first in Seattle, then in Portland, and even in Boise, Idaho. He married Aunty Sol (Eskenazy) in 1912; they lived in Portland for some time, and then by the 1940s they moved permanently to Seattle.

Uncle Ralph worked hard to earn enough money to bring his sisters to the United States. First he brought his sister, Calo, who married and settled in Portland. Later, he enabled his other sisters—including Nona—to come to Seattle.

I remember Uncle Ralph as a remarkably dignified man. He seemed always to be well dressed. He smoked cigars. He looked like he could have been a president of a bank or a CEO of a big company. He and Aunty Sol bought a home on 31st Avenue with a phenomenal view of Lake Washington. Uncle Ralph would sit on his rocking chair near the window, smoke a cigar, sip a cup of Turkish coffee, and enjoy the view.

He and Aunty Sol planted vegetables in a grass strip in the middle of the driveway to their house. They did not drive, so the driveway was put to good use.

Uncle Ralph was punctual, meticulous and had a strong sense of responsibility for his family. He had a lively sense of humor and often enjoyed a good laugh with his cousin Ike Eskenazy. Ike, also from Marmara, was hilarious when he told stories and laughed uproariously at his own jokes.

With Uncle Ralph's assistance, his sister Sultana travelled to

Seattle with a group of friends from Marmara. Among the group was Bohora Rousso who was going to Seattle to marry a man she had never met. The marriage had been arranged by the parents. The group travelled by ship to New York, and then by train to Seattle.

Bohora's fiancé, Mordecai Coronel, came to meet her at the train station, bringing along his cousin Marco Romey. Bohora met her husband-to-be and both were very pleased. That was also the first time that my grandparents, Marco Romey and Sultana Policar, met. They immediately fell in love and were married on May 23, 1912.

As mentioned earlier, some Sephardim of Seattle had moved to Portland and established a community there. Among the Sephardim of Portland were my Nona's older sister Calo, Calo's husband Isaac, and various relatives.

I remember our family traveling to Portland one summer in order to visit Aunty Calo. I was just a little boy and had never been to her home before. Nor had I ever met her children. As we approached Portland on the highway, Mom turned to the back seat of the car where we children were sitting. She had a serious expression on her face. "We are going to visit Aunty Calo. She has two children living at home with her. I want you to behave yourselves and act natural. The children are midgets."

"Midgets?" I called out in surprise. I didn't know whether to be excited or to be afraid about meeting real midgets.

"They are just like all other human beings, only smaller," Mom continued. "They will feel self-conscious if you treat them in a strange way. Just act natural. Aunty Calo has enough suffering; she doesn't need us to make more problems."

For the remainder of the ride, we were all silent. We each had to think carefully about our forthcoming visit and how we would just act natural.

As Dad drove the car into Aunty Calo's driveway, I felt my heart sink. My older brother Bill had already been to Aunty Calo's house in the past; he was calm. My sister Bernice, being even younger than I, seemed oblivious to the experience before us. I kept repeating Mom's instructions in my mind: act natural.

Aunty Calo greeted us at the door. She was very round—a round face, a round body. To me, even her teeth seemed round. She smiled and laughed with genuine happiness. She hugged each of us and asked us many questions without waiting for answers.

Within a few minutes, we were sitting around her kitchen table. Aunty served Turkish coffee to my parents, and poured glasses of milk for the children. The table was laden with sweets and home-baked pastries like my grandmother baked. I actually started to feel at home and act natural.

But the thought of the midgets lingered in my mind. Where were they? When would we see them? Are they afraid of us? Will I vomit when I first see them? I sat at the table pretending to be natural; but I was filled with dread and confusion.

A few minutes passed. We were stuffing ourselves with Aunty Calo's goodies as she was chatting away and laughing. She was constantly hugging and kissing us. I kept thinking: where are the midgets? Would they hug and kiss me too?

A few more minutes passed. I started to hope that the midgets would not show up. Maybe they were taking a nap, maybe they weren't even home. Maybe Aunty Calo was hiding them away because she was ashamed of them.

After we finished eating, we went into the living room. I tugged at my mother's dress: can we go now? She smiled sternly and told me to behave myself and act natural.

And then it happened. We heard footsteps from the hall staircase. In an instant, David and Esther were in the room with us. In spite of myself, I shuddered.

They were short, wide and bow-legged. They looked though they had been squashed and compressed by a powerful machine. It was impossible to guess how old they were, although my mother told us they were in their late twenties. When they spoke, they sounded something like Donald Duck. Esther was wearing a lovely party dress and patent leather Mary Jane shoes. David was dressed in slacks and a fashionable V-neck sweater. They were smiling. They came to each of us, shook our hands, and showed real pleasure in welcoming us. I still remember the squeamish feeling I had when I shook their hands.

As Esther and David were greeting us, my eyes shot toward Aunty Calo. She was not ashamed of them at all. She was beaming with pride and happiness.

"Now," Aunty Calo announced, "Esther and David will take the children upstairs to play for a while."

My brother and sister followed right along as the midgets went upstairs. I sidled up to my mother, but she quickly and as inconspicuously as possible shoved me toward the steps. I took a deep breath and followed the others upstairs.

We went into David's room. He showed us some toys and jigsaw puzzles. He really tried hard to be natural. He was a wonderful conversationalist. Both he and Esther were quite intelligent and spent a lot of time reading. We actually were all having a good time together. I thought that I was acting natural; but apparently David sensed my unease. He pulled me aside and whispered into my ear: "Don't worry about us. We are happy. We don't feel sorry for ourselves, so you shouldn't feel sorry for us either." The words pierced through me.

Our visit finally came to a close. We all hugged and kissed Aunty Calo, Esther and David. We got back into the car, and Dad started the engine. We were going to Seaside, Oregon, for a short vacation. It was one of our favorite places. Usually, when we were on the way to Seaside, we children would be singing, fighting, screaming and otherwise expressing our excitement. This time, we were quiet.

"Did I do okay?" I finally asked my mother

"You were all fine," she said to the children. "You were all as natural as you could be."

"It was kind of fun," I said weakly.

"We'll visit them again one day," my mother responded.

I was glad. But I shuddered.

Within the next several years, both Esther and David died. Although I had only met them that one time, I cried when I learned of their deaths. Mom told me that I would get over the sadness.

Many, many years have passed. But the sadness remains.

Nissim was born in Turkey and came to Seattle as a young man. He was short, energetic and had a very loud voice.

Nissim taught me how to tie the tsitsith—ritual fringes placed on four-cornered garments—according to the practice of the Sephardim of Turkey. He showed me how to loop the tsitsith strings in a pattern of ten, five, six, five, the numbers that represent the Hebrew letters constituting the name of God. He also taught me how to tie the knots of the tefillin, leather boxes and straps that men wear during morning daily prayers. The boxes contain parchments with Biblical verses, reminding us to worship God with our mind (intellect), heart (emotion) and arms (actions).

Nissim taught me how to hold my hand over my eyes during the recitation of the Shema prayer. The five fingers of the right hand are so arranged as to form three Hebrew letters that spell Shaddai, one of God's names in Hebrew. One morning, Nissim rushed into synagogue with an extra burst of energy. He pulled out of his pocket a newspaper article about a certain prominent politician. The article was accompanied by a photograph of the politician—a man of impeccable WASP heritage—that caught him at a pensive moment. The photo showed him holding his right hand over his eyes, and his fingers were arranged precisely the way we do when we recite the Shema. Nissim put the photo close to my face: "You see," he told me with delight, "this politician is obviously Jewish. He is saying the Shema. Who would have guessed?" It is unlikely that the politician realized how much hidden meaning there was in this photo of him!

Nissim's religious nature included a profound love for the land of Israel. I remember him telling me how fortunate we were to be living in an era when the holy land had been restored to the Jewish people. He and his wife had travelled to Israel after it had officially been established as a modern state. The memory of that visit stayed with him. It grew into a longing to return to Israel, to live there, and ultimately to die there.

As the years passed, Nissim's yearning for Israel intensified. He told me: "Israel is God's gift to the Jewish people. It is our sacred land since antiquity. We live in a miraculous age when God has given the land back to our people."

Nissim wanted to move to Israel, to live in Jerusalem, to dwell in its holiness. This was a religious ideal that quietly and steadily burned within him. But his wife did not share that dream. Her family and friends lived in Seattle. She had spent most of her life here. How was she now, at her advanced age, to become an immigrant? How could she hope to learn a new language, adapt to a new way of life?

"Nissim," she told him, "Seattle is our home. We have everyone we love here, everything we need here. Let us visit Israel, even stay there for a month or two. But at our age, it makes no sense to leave home and start all over again somewhere else."

To which Nissim would have replied: "Israel is our real home. Seattle has only been a rest stop along the way. Israel is the home of our people and that's where we belong." Instead of offering this reply, he accepted his wife's words with silent resignation. He would not settle in Jerusalem without her; and she was not ready to make the move.

At some point, Nissim and his wife took a car trip to California. They were involved in a serious accident and his wife was injured badly. She never fully recovered; she died some months later. She was buried in the Sephardic cemetery in Seattle.

Nissim was somber and heartbroken. As a sign of mourning, he let his beard grow, white and full. His eyes were deeper, his voice softer. He looked like he could have been one of the ancient prophets of Israel.

Months past. Then Nissim announced that he was going to move to Jerusalem. He arranged to have his wife disinterred from the cemetery in Seattle and transferred to a cemetery in Israel. He suddenly became re-energized. His eyes grew brighter, his voice stronger. He was at last going to fulfill his dream of moving to Jerusalem.

When he left Seattle, he was crying. He had long wanted to settle in Jerusalem with his wife. Now he was going there to bury her. And to spend his last years waiting to join her in the Jerusalem on high.

Among the regular guests at my grandparents' home each Shabbat afternoon were Uncle Morris and Aunty Esther. Aunty was Nona's sister. The two of them were very devoted to each other. When Nona was ill—which was often—Aunty Esther would visit her and try to lift her spirits.

Aunty Esther, like Aunty Calo, was round. Everything about her seemed round—no angles, nothing jarring. She laughed heartily and often. She exuded a spirit of goodwill and honesty.

Uncle Morris was a sturdy, handsome man, born on the Island of Rhodes. He was always at Aunty Esther's side. Papoo used to excuse himself early on Shabbat afternoons in order to go upstairs and take his Sabbath nap. Uncle Morris would then be left as the only adult male in a room full of women and children. He never seemed to mind. He participated actively in the discussions, complained about the many injustices in the world, laughed at funny stories.

My mother and us children would walk to Nona and Papoo's house almost every Saturday after lunch. Occasionally, Dad would join us, although his normal pattern was to devote the afternoon to his Shabbat nap.

I grew up expecting to see Uncle Morris and Aunty Esther together at my grandparents' home on Shabbat afternoons. This is how things were for years.

At some point, though, their attendance at the Shabbat afternoon gatherings began to decline. At first, they missed a Shabbat every now and then; but soon, the absences grew more frequent.

I asked Mom why they did not come to visit Nona as much as before. "Aunty Esther has not been feeling well."

"What's wrong with her?" I asked.

"They don't know."

This information—or lack of information—weighed heavily on me. They didn't know! How could she be cured if they didn't even know what was wrong with her?

When Uncle Morris and Aunty Esther did appear at Nona's house on some Shabbat afternoons, I stared at her as inconspicuously as I could, to see if I could detect what was wrong with her. She looked a bit pale, less round than usual. Her joviality was somewhat diminished. But all in all, she seemed to be mostly alright.

As the weeks proceeded, her condition obviously deteriorated. Her eyes seemed to be gazing at something far away. Her conversation drifted. She started to forget our names. One could see from Uncle Morris's expression that something was seriously amiss. He was as devoted to her as ever; but his face showed the strains of prolonged anguish.

Nona observed with sadness the gradual transformation of her beloved sister. Aunty Esther looked almost the same on the outside. But her mind was going. Day by day, her memory was slipping away. Little by little, she stopped recognizing us.

Aunty Esther's face continued to smile, out of habit. She laughed, but didn't seem to know why she was laughing. Her face was the same, but her mind was not the same.

Nona had stoical tendencies. She tried to accept Aunty Esther's illness with equanimity, hoping that it would be cured. There was to be no cure. As this reality sank into Nona's consciousness, she mourned the loss of her sister. For although Aunty Esther's body was still intact, her memory had died; she was now only an image of who she had been.

Eliyahu and Reyna Romey, photo taken in Tekirdag,
Turkey, late 19th century

Marco and Sultana Romey (author's maternal grandparents) with their
children. left to right, Regina, David (sitting on the stool) Leo, Estreya and
Rachel (author's mother)

Family group, taken in Rhodes c. 1911. Bulissa Esther Angel (author's grand-mother) is at the center of the photo, surrounded by her children, and some neighbor children. On the bottom row, far right, wearing a fez, is Joseph...who wasn't allowed entry into the US and had to return to Rhodes while the rest of the family went on to Seattle.

Rachel and Victor Angel at the time of their engagement

Rachel and Victor Angel, wedding photo

A "visita": left to right: Rachel Altabet, Rachel Angel (standing), Victoria
Franco, Sultana Romey and Marc Angel (the author)

Aunty Esther lived on for a number of years, with Uncle Morris and family devoting themselves to caring for her.

Some people die suddenly. Some die after a protracted illness. Aunty Esther seemed to have died by gradually fading away.

Aunty Kadun, another of Nona's sisters, was beautiful, stately and elegant. She dressed well, tending to the side of formality. She had a very dry sense of humor and would often not laugh at things that seemed funny to everyone else. It became an informal game among us to see if we could get Aunty Kadun to laugh. We usually lost.

Like her sisters, Aunty Kadun was born in Marmara and had come to Seattle as a teenager. She lacked formal education but was highly intelligent. Her mind was alert and retentive. She knew a great many things.

She did not have an easy life. Nevertheless, she would not let herself be crushed by adversity. Her inner pride and grace helped her to overcome many troubles.

Aunty Kadun was a lady of style and moral seriousness. She believed that good people did not use curse words. When she became angry, she would nod her head in perplexity, or would mutter the words "Sacramento California" in a tone of voice that sounded as though she were cursing. As a little boy, I thought "Sacramento California" was a swear word.

She did not approve of women wearing pants, immodest dresses or swim suits. Mothers should behave like mothers; and grandmothers like grandmothers. These were serious roles, requiring modesty and decency. Children who grew up seeing their mothers dressed immodestly would lose respect for their mothers; they would not grow up to be good parents themselves.

Aunty Kadun was very sensitive to breezes. Whenever she

came to our house, we had to close the windows. If she was in the car with us, the windows remained closed no matter how hot and stuffy it became. She usually wore a sweater or long sleeved dress, even in the summer.

She was frequently at our home. It was customary for the ladies in our community to have visitas, little social gatherings, from time to time. They would invite a few of their relatives and friends, and would prepare a wonderful array of baked goods and sweets. My mother invariably would invite Aunty Kadun to the visitas at our house.

Although these gatherings were not held to commemorate any special occasion, they were treated with a certain degree of formality. The hostess baked everything that was to be served; to offer store-bought goods was tactless and disrespectful. The food was served on the best set of dishes. The hostess and guests dressed up nicely and would not think of wearing something casual or informal.

Women would host visitas whenever the mood struck them, or whenever they felt they had to repay social obligations. One of the visitas hosted by my mother came about in an unusual way. Mom received a telephone call from a woman who said she wanted to stop by for a visit. The voice was friendly and warm. It spoke in Spanish, meaning that the caller was someone from the older generation. Spontaneously, Mom invited her to a visita the following week.

After hanging up the phone, Mom started to make up a list of people to invite. The only problem was that she had not recognized the voice of the woman who had called her! She was too embarrassed to ask the caller to identify herself.

Mom called Aunty Kadun. "We are having a visita at my house next week. We have a mystery guest. Will you be able to attend?"

Aunty Kadun, who had little patience with practical jokes, retorted: "Rachel (Rashelle, as she pronounced it), what do you mean 'a mystery guest?' Enough of this nonsense. Who is coming to the visita?"

"I really don't know, Aunty."

"Maybe I don't like your mystery guest. Maybe I won't come unless you tell me who she is."

"Honestly, Aunty, I don't know. It will be a surprise for all of us."

"Asi biva yo (as I live), I think you are playing a game with me. You shouldn't tease your elders."

During the week before the visita, Aunty Kadun called my mother several times to find out the identity of the mystery guest. She was reluctant to attend a social gathering where she might meet someone she did not particularly like.

When the day of the visita came, Aunty Kadun was the first to arrive. My mother told her not to show any surprise when the mystery guest arrived. She wanted the guest to feel remembered and loved. It would be embarrassing if she ever were to find out the real story behind this visita.

As the guests arrived, Aunty Kadun remained a bit distant and ill at ease. Soon enough, though, the mystery guest appeared—an old friend of the family whom Aunty Kadun liked very much. The afternoon turned out to be a great success. When the visita was over, Aunty Kadun remained for a few minutes after the other guests had left.

"I tell you, Rachel, it was a lovely party. But you nearly gave me an ulcer. All week I was torturing myself about whether or not I would know or like your mystery guest, or whether you were just playing a game with me." Then she gave Mom a classic Aunty Kadun compliment: "Even though you almost killed me, it was a nice visita."

This reminded Mom of another compliment she had received from Aunty Kadun: "Rachel, you are very demure, you hardly eat anything. And yet, you are not slender!"

Aunty Kadun's personality showed itself in another episode. Mom had planted squash in a vegetable patch in our back yard. The squash grew amazingly well. One of them reached an exceptionally large size, and Mom took a snapshot of it with her Brownie camera. When the film was developed, Mom placed the photograph on the mantle over the fireplace in the living room, next to an assortment of family photographs.

On one of her visits to our home, Aunty Kadun found herself in the living room looking at the pictures on the mantle. Being a bit nearsighted, she gazed wonderingly at the picture of the squash, not quite able to recognize who it was.

"Rachel, who is in this picture?"

My mother laughed. "It's my calavasa (squash), Aunty."

Aunty Kadun gave my mother one of her famous cynical glances. "Why are you teasing me? I asked you a simple question, so you should answer me. Who is the baby in the picture?"

"Really, Aunty. It's my calavasa."

"Don't be silly. No one takes pictures of a calavasa and puts it on the mantle among family photos."

"But that is exactly what I did. The calavasa grew so large, I wanted to take a picture of it. I'm very proud of it."

Aunty Kadun removed her glasses and held the photograph close to her eyes. "Asi biva yo, Rachel, this is a picture of a calavasa!"

She looked at Mom who had begun to laugh. And then even Aunty Kadun had a good laugh.

As the years passed, Aunty Kadun retained her vigorous health, energy and dignity. She seemed timeless, changeless. She gave the impression of being immune to aging and dying. However, this illusion finally gave way. Her health declined and she felt she could no longer care for herself in her own apartment. Arrangements were made for her to become a resident of the Kline Galland Home for the Aged, the Jewish community's nursing home. She still would come out from time to time for visits; but these occasions grew less frequent.

When Aunty Kadun died in 1975, this marked the end of a generation in our family. She was the last of Nona's siblings to pass away. I somehow thought that Aunty Kadun's funeral would be marked by a dramatic public ceremony marking the end of a generation. But there was only a simple funeral for a good woman.

Part III

The First American-Born Generation

Mom was the second-born child of her parents. The first-born was her sister Regina. The third-born was her brother Leo, followed later by Estreya, David, Sarah and Esther. Mom's position in the family was to influence her entire life.

In those days, parents (or at least fathers) wanted to have sons. While sons were welcomed with joy and pride, daughters were accepted with resignation. Mom once told me that her sister Regina, even though "only" a girl, had the advantage of being first-born. But when Mom was born, the second consecutive daughter, this was somehow unforgivable. When Leo came along, parental affection went to the new son.

Being second-born and a girl, Mom was sandwiched between two siblings whose births had elicited greater enthusiasm than hers. While very much loved and well-treated by her parents, she started life by feeling that she was not special.

We have a family photograph of my grandparents and their first five children. Mom, at the time, was about ten years old. Papoo is standing in the center of the picture holding Leo's hand. Regina is next to her mother. Estreya is standing at the left corner of the picture. David, who is just a child of two or three years old, sits on a highchair in the foreground. Off to the right stands Mom. She is not smiling. She does not look angry or upset, but neither does she appear to be happy. In her eyes, one sees a kind of youthful melancholy, an introspectiveness. She learned the philosophy of resignation and acceptance. One of her pet phrases throughout life was: "No one said that life is fair. You have to make the best of things."

The family was poor. It was not possible for Papoo to buy fashionable new clothes for his children. Their wardrobes were simple—a few plain things for during the week, and a fancier outfit for the Sabbath. Used clothes, like used furniture for the house, were not unusual.

When Mom needed a new pair of shoes, Papoo would put his hand against her foot to get an idea as to her size. He would then find a peddler who sold shoes and would pick out a pair that he calculated would fit Mom. Whether they fit or not—and they usually did not—those became Mom's shoes until she wore them out completely. When the soles of the shoes had holes, she learned to stuff the shoes with pieces of newspaper in order to keep out the wet and cold.

In recollecting the agony of her feet during childhood, Mom generally laughed about her past suffering. "We were poor. I had no right to expect a fine pair of shoes. I was lucky to have anything at all to protect my feet. That's how life was in those days."

When Mom was enrolled in public school at age five, she did not know how to speak English. The language at home and in the society in which she lived was Judeo-Spanish. When she went to school, she was like an immigrant although she had been born and raised in Seattle.

While struggling to adapt to public school, she had other trials to face. She was a red-head. Some classmates teased her, calling her "carrot top." She became self-conscious about her hair and felt the excruciating pain of being ridiculed by peers.

She was an extremely bright student, quickly mastering English and all her subjects. She loved to read. Her budding academic skills received little encouragement at home. After all, she was "only" a girl; girls did not need formal education. They needed to learn how to be good wives and mothers, things that could be best learned at home. Sending girls to school was simply a concession to life in America.

Mom did well in school. My grandparents had also enrolled her in an afterschool religious program where she learned to read Hebrew and studied Bible.

At home, she learned important skills from her mother: how to sew, embroider, crochet and knit. She learned cooking and the laws of keeping a kosher home. She helped Nona make jams and preserves. She memorized the prayers and blessings that women needed to know.

On Friday afternoons, before the onset of the Sabbath, she helped Nona make wicks for the lampara (oil lamp) that was lit in honor of Shabbat. This was done by breaking small pieces of straw from the bottom of a broom, and wrapping them in a thin layer of cotton. These wicks were then inserted into a round metal holder that was placed in a large glass bowl. The bowl would be filled about half way with water, and above the water would be a layer of several inches of vegetable oil. The wicks were lit about twenty minutes before sunset each Friday afternoon, and this is when the women of the house began their observance of the Sabbath.

During her school years, Mom and her siblings were responsible for household chores. They helped clean the house; bring in the wood and coal for the stove; do the laundry by hand and then hang it on clotheslines in the backyard or basement to dry; tend the yard and vegetable garden. Nona was not blessed with vigorous strength or robust health; she relied on her children, especially her older daughters, to help.

Mom was called upon to assist in caring for her younger siblings. One night, she and her sister Regina were babysitting for the five younger children. The youngest—and most troublesome—was Esther. Somehow, little Esther managed to get hold of a pin. She carried it to her older sisters, threatening to swallow it if they did not accede to one of her demands. They screamed at her to drop the pin, but within an instant Esther put it into her mouth and swallowed it. This was followed by her howls of pain. The older sisters did not know what to do. They shook her, slapped her back, tried to get her to vomit. Crying Esther told them: "If I die it will be your fault."

While Regina was on the phone calling for help, Mom solemnly warned Esther: "Don't you dare die until Mama gets home." Miraculously, Esther survived and continued to give her sisters much excitement for years to come.

Leo could be a problem at times. One day, he hammered a bunch of nails into the wall alongside the staircase, and left the nails protruding from the wall. As it happened, Papoo, who made his own wine in those days, needed to carry a tub of wine down the steps. His pants caught onto the nails; he lost balance and fell down the stairs. Fortunately, he was not hurt too badly…but the wine had spilled and was ruined.

When Nona wanted a reprieve from her children, she would send them on an errand to the home of a relative or friend. She would tell them go and get a teneme aki (keep me here). When the woman to whose house they were sent heard this message, she would tell the children to sit down for a while until she could find it. Then a stall tactic ensued in which the children were kept waiting for an hour or two. At last, they were given a closed bag and told to return home. They were also given some candy as a reward for their patience.

Mom never had a store-bought doll as a child, since dolls were an unnecessary expense. She and her sisters made their own dolls by stringing together empty spools of thread. As a special diversion, the children went to the movies, walking downtown to the Florence or Gem theater. For five cents admission, they would spend the day at the movies. Nona would pack them a lunch, and off they went.

As she grew older, Mom's formal education continued at Garfield High School. She excelled in her studies; she loved her classes. Her social life revolved around her relatives and Sephardic friends; but the public school experience enabled her to develop a broader range of acquaintances.

She once reminisced: "In those days it didn't matter if you were Jewish or Christian or black or Japanese or anything else. Everyone got along, everyone tried to blend in. When the Jewish kids stayed home for Jewish holidays, a lot of our non-Jewish friends would also take the day off school. In those days there was no militancy, no radicalism in our school."

Shortly before she reached her sixteenth birthday, Papoo told her that she would have to leave school once she turned sixteen so that she could get a job and help with the family expenses. Her older sister, Regina, had already left school to go to work. Mom was deeply pained, but she accepted her father's decree with a sense of fatalism. There was really no choice for her, so why fight or struggle against the inevitable?

She notified the school administration and her teachers that she would be leaving school once she turned sixteen. Many of them sought to convince her not to drop out. Mom remembered with fondness that one of her teachers, Mrs. Ryan, called Papoo to plead with him to leave his daughter in school. She was an excellent student with a bright future. But this request made no sense in the context of my grandfather's life. He was a poor man. He had a wife and seven children to support. The family needed every dollar that could be brought in. Education for girls was a frivolous luxury that he could not afford.

So Mom left Garfield and went to work at the Parisian Candy Factory with her sister Regina. They earned 32 cents per hour, almost all of which they contributed to the family income. Although Mom regretted having to leave school, she never expressed resentment against her father. "It was not his fault. It was the way he was raised, the way he was taught to deal with life. We were poor. We needed my income."

I once began a conversation with Mom wondering what her life would have been like had she been born a generation or two later. "You would have had the chance to receive a university education. You could have become a great writer or teacher or public figure or…"

She cut off my line of conversation with a smile. "It is a waste of time to imagine what would have been. I can only live my life as it has been given to me. All in all, it has been a good and happy life. I am grateful to God."

Throughout her life, she was a voracious reader. Her literary interests were broad and eclectic. In spite of her lack of a high school diploma or university degree, she was a highly educated person.

After Mom's death, I was discussing her life with one of my cousins. I mentioned that Mom had never graduated high school. My cousin, who knew my mother well, was stunned. "I had always thought that your mother was a college graduate."

Mom would have blushed.

Dad was the only American-born child of his parents. Although he did not visit the Island of Rhodes until he was in his sixties, he was raised in many ways as though he had been born there. The language of his home and society was Judeo-Spanish, with the distinctive pronunciation of Rhodes Jews.

His mother was a forward-looking woman who wanted her children to adapt well to life in America. She was especially eager for her American-born baby to be modern and progressive. Yet, even in this regard, modernity was supposed to go hand in hand with traditional cultural patterns. For example, Nona Angel was under the impression that American children were supposed to learn to play a musical instrument. Even though there was little money to spare, she arranged for Dad to take violin lessons. He was only nine or ten at the time but was enthusiastic about this special opportunity.

He took his lessons seriously and practiced conscientiously.

His mother was proud of her young musical prodigy. Whenever she had guests at her home, she would call on him to give a recital on his violin. He played the pieces he had learned from his music teacher. The guests were impressed; but then they would ask him to play some Turkish or Judeo-Spanish songs. Of course, Dad could not play well enough to meet these requests; he became embarrassed and frustrated. My grandmother came to think of the lessons as a waste of money; if her son could not play the Turkish and Sephardic songs, what was the point of learning to play the violin? The music teacher told her that it would take years before Dad would gain the proficiency to play the music she wanted. That settled the matter: no more money wasted on violin lessons!

Dad was thin and frail as a child and was susceptible to colds. To protect him, his mother dressed him warmly. He wore her hand-knitted sweaters all year long, even in the warm weather. When Dad grew older, he rebelled. For many years, he refused to wear sweaters. He preferred to wear short sleeved shirts, even in winter.

The calamity of his childhood was the death of his father. At the time, Dad was twelve years old. Only his brother Ray and he were still living at home with their mother; the older brothers and sisters were already married and on their own. Ray was about four years older than Dad.

Papoo Angel left very little in the way of financial assets. The house still had a mortgage. My grandmother earned a bit from those who came to her for cures, but this was not nearly enough to meet the ongoing expenses of the household. Her married children had problems of their own and were not able to add much to her income. Thus, the responsibility fell mainly on Dad and Ray. In spite of their youth, they had no choice but to rise to the challenge. They did.

Dad was proud of the fact that he and Ray were able to earn enough to buy a radio for their mother in 1927. Nona Angel thus became one of the few people in the community who had a real radio, not just a crystal set with earphones.

We have a photograph of my father taken when he was thirteen years old, on the day his mother made a luncheon in honor of his Bar Mitzvah. That morning, she had sent him to synagogue and told him to tell the sexton that this was the day of his Bar Mitzvah. Dad's religious instruction up to that point had been rudimentary. He hardly knew what it meant to be Bar Mitzvah, to have come of age to be responsible for fulfilling the laws and traditions of Judaism. Some old men at the synagogue congratulated him on his Bar Mitzvah. They wrapped him in a prayer shawl and tefillin, and had him called to the Torah. After the services, they again congratulated him, removed the prayer shawl and tefillin…and that was it. Dad left for home without having understood what had transpired.

Later that morning, relatives and friends of the family came to the luncheon his mother had prepared in his honor. He received a few presents, a few hugs and kisses. His mother made a fuss over him, praising his virtues.

In the Bar Mitzvah photograph, Dad is—of course—wearing a heavy knit sweater, even though it was a nice spring day in April. He also is sporting a wrist watch that had been given to him in honor of the occasion. Looking at the photograph many years later, Dad commented that the day of his Bar Mitzvah had mystified him. He had no preparation for it and did not know exactly what it was supposed to mean. He was grateful to his mother for having gone to the trouble of making a luncheon for him and for allowing him to skip school that day. And yet, he long felt that he had not had a real Bar Mitzvah. When his own sons and grandsons had their Bar Mitzvah ceremonies, Dad enjoyed those events as though he himself were finally celebrating his own Bar Mitzvah.

When it was time for High School, Dad was enrolled in Garfield. He was a good student and managed to find time to participate as a writer for the school newspaper. All in all, he was an affable, popular student, known for his lively sense of humor. Throughout his life, he retained pride and loyalty for Garfield and was an avid fan of its sports teams.

Upon graduation from Garfield, Dad sought a full time job.

Going to college was out of the question. There was neither money nor time for such a luxury. He had been working part time for relatives who owned a fruit stand. He decided to seek work in that occupation since he had some experience in it.

This was the era of the great economic depression in the United States. Money and jobs were scarce. Poverty was rampant. For people who were already poor, the depression made matters even worse.

Dad was determined not to be poor. He would work as long and as hard as necessary to be able to live at a good standard of living. While he would not have minded becoming rich, his goal was always to be self-sufficient and independent.

Dad joined his brother Ray and several cousins in operating a fruit stand in the old Broadway Market. Dad and Ray did well enough to buy a car. Dad liked the food business, because people always had to eat…even during depressions.

Within several years, Dad opened a new fruit and vegetable stand with one of his cousins. He was working hard, earning money, and was turning his thoughts to getting married and starting a family of his own.

Meeting Mom was the great turning point in his life.

Mom had a very close relationship with her mother and considered her to be the epitome of goodness, wisdom, gracefulness and compassion. Even though Nona had been born in Turkey, had received little formal education and could not even speak English, she was strikingly alert to the modern trends and to the concerns and needs of her American-born children.

Mom sought her mother's advice on a matter that was to determine the course of her life.

While attending one of the dances sponsored by the Sephar-

Marc D. Angel

dic community, Mom met a young man named Victor Angel. Although he lived only about seven blocks from her, the two of them were not acquainted with each other. He was part of the community of Rhodes Jews and she was part of the community of Turkish Jews; in those days, the two groups did not often intermingle. On that night, though, he asked her to dance. They immediately liked each other and had a nice evening together. When Mom returned home, she told Nona that she had met a very nice young man. Nona obviously saw from my mother's expression that she was very taken with him. She advised her to go to the next dance also, and to get to know the young man a bit better.

Mom did go to the next dance; but Victor was not there. She was crestfallen. Perhaps he didn't really like her; perhaps he already had a girlfriend; perhaps he did not want to see her again. Mustering as much courage as she could, she went across the dance floor to a young man who was a friend of Victor. As casually as possible—and pretending not to be really interested—she inquired about Victor's whereabouts. The friend responded: "Victor is extremely ill; he may even die. He's in the hospital."

Badly shaken, Mom struggled to maintain a calm veneer. "I'm so sorry to hear that. I hope he feels better soon."

She left the dance shortly thereafter and came home crying. She went to her mother to have a confidential conversation.

Mom told Nona that she had learned about Victor's being hospitalized with a serious illness. Nona commiserated with her. Then my mother made a strange request: "Would it be alright if I visited him in the hospital?"

Even as she asked the question, she knew that she was requesting something that was not proper. A young woman simply did not visit a young man, certainly not one whom she hardly even knew. Such an act would be considered to be brazen, immodest. Propriety demanded that the man go after the woman, not vice versa. Mom, a shy and modest young lady, knew this all too well. And yet she asked.

Nona was perceptive enough to understand that if Mom asked

76

such a question—so much out of character for her—then she must indeed have had deep feelings for the young man. Nona responded: "You go to see him in the hospital tomorrow."

Mom was heartened, but still afraid. "But it is not really proper. And what will Pa say if he learns about this?"

Nona hugged her daughter. "Rachel, you go visit the young man in the hospital tomorrow. Don't worry about what anyone else will say. And don't worry about your father, I'll see to it that he understands the situation."

The next day, after work at the candy factory, Mom went to Providence Hospital to visit a young man she hardly knew. She had learned that he was suffering from a bad case of pneumonia. He was having difficulty breathing. The prognosis for his recovery was uncertain.

She entered his hospital room and saw him lying on his back, looking miserable and forlorn. Upon hearing footsteps in the room, he painfully turned toward the door. He saw the young lady he had recently met at the dance. He broke into a broad smile.

She apologized for intruding. He reassured her and thanked her. The visit lasted for only a few minutes; but it changed both of their lives forever.

Within a few days, Victor Angel made an amazing recovery from his illness. Within a few weeks, he was released from the hospital. Within a few months, he and Mom were engaged to be married. As long as he lived, Dad maintained that Mom's visit to him had cured him from his illness; he owed her his life.

For all his dash and charm, Dad was shy when it came to proposing marriage. He decided to write her a letter in which he proposed to Mom. He mailed the letter to her, care of the Parisian Candy Factory. On the day he assumed the letter would have arrived, he met her as she was leaving work. They smiled. She told him that she had received his letter…and the answer was yes. Happiness!

When Dad first met my Mom's parents, there were a few moments of tension. My grandparents did not know my father's family. Papoo suspected that my father might have been an Americano, a word used to designate a non-Jewish young man. My father teased my grandfather by agreeing that he was an Americano, since he was in fact born in America. But once Mom's parents met Dad's mother, everything was set straight. A wedding date was set—May 23, 1937. That date also was the twenty-fifth anniversary of my Mom's parents.

Papoo took my father aside for a confidential talk. He told his future son-in-law that he was a poor barber and could not afford to give his daughter a dowry. Dad, who had not at all expected a dowry, reassured Papoo that he wanted nothing from him except permission to marry his daughter Rachel. The two men shook hands and became wonderful friends.

Among the Sephardim of that generation, it was customary for the groom's side to arrange and pay for the wedding. Thus, the wedding took place in the synagogue of Dad's family, Ezra Bessaroth. Papoo, who was a staunch leader of the Sephardic Bikur Holim, was less than enthusiastic about his daughter being married at Ezra Bessaroth. Wisely, though, he deferred to the prevailing custom without objection. To maintain his Turkish Sephardic honor, he saw to it that the two witnesses for the marriage contract were members of the Bikur Holim.

Shortly after my parents' engagement, Dad's older brother Ray became engaged. His fiancée felt that it would be appropriate if she and Ray were married before my parents, since Ray was older than Victor. My parents, though, felt that they had priority since they had been engaged first and had already set the date for their wedding. The matter was settled by Nona Angel.

La Gremma knew the traditions well, and she knew that older siblings were given priority to their younger siblings. In this case, Ray's engagement came only a bit later than Victor's and by normal rules of tradition, Ray should have precedence. But La Gremma had a strong sense of justice. She decided that Victor was engaged first, so Victor should be married first. The tradition would have to bend to the dictates of fairness. Perhaps she also had a special appreciation for my mother, whose boldness had saved her son's life. La Gremma decided: and so it was.

In those days, wedding invitations were not printed and mailed to invitees. Rather, the families of the bride and groom made up a list of people they wished to invite. They then hired the synagogue's sexton who would go from house to house to invite the guests. "Mrs. Bulissa Esther Angel and Mr. and Mrs. Marco Romey will be honored if you would join them for the wedding of their children Victor Angel and Rachel Romey, to take place on May 23 at Ezra Bessaroth." The guests responded on the spot—no need for RSVP's.

While the groom's family had the responsibility of arranging the wedding and reception, the bride's family also had obligations. The main one was providing the ashugar, the trousseau. Daughters began preparing their ashugar almost as soon as they learned to sew and crochet. Mothers started preparing from the moment they gave birth to a daughter.

The ashugar included linens, bedding, and articles of clothing. The items were crocheted, embroidered and knitted. Families took pride in the elegance of the daughter's trousseau—the quality of the materials, the craftsmanship of the embroidery, the decorativeness of the patterns. The week before Mom's wedding, relatives and friends came to my grandparents' home where the items of the ashugar were on display. The guests expressed their praise and approval, and were treated to sweets and Turkish coffee. Every day during that week was filled with guests and partying.

Gifts of food were sent from the family of the groom to the family of the bride. These gifts were reciprocated. Each side tried to provide wonderful baked goods and sweets that would be enjoyed by their soon-to-be-joined families.

The night before the wedding, Mom was brought to the banyo, the ritual bath. She was accompanied by her mother, sisters, aunties and other female relatives and friends. As she emerged from her immersion in the water, Nona gently broke a rosca (a round baked pastry) over Mom's head as a sign of blessing. The women expressed their good wishes, sang traditional Judeo-Spanish wedding songs, and enjoyed refreshments that Nona had provided.

The wedding was, of course, conducted according to the Sephardic traditions. As the participants in the wedding procession walked down the aisle, a group of men sang Hebrew songs, accompanied by an oud. Following the ceremony, the guests were served a home-made meal, topped off with a vast array of Sephardic sweets and deserts prepared by the women of both families. People sang and danced to Judeo-Spanish and Turkish music.

What could be happier than a wedding? And yet, sometimes people cry at weddings. From where do these tears stem? Are they merely tears of joy?

Certainly, the tears come from the wellsprings of happiness. But they also derive from other sources: melancholy at the passing of time; fear of change and transition; anxiety about the future. Mom had her set of concerns. She and Dad, in spite of the similarity of their cultural backgrounds, belonged to two different communities. Mom grew up among Turkish Jews, Dad among Jews from Rhodes. These two communities in Seattle maintained separate identities, with each group feeling a certain aloofness from the other.

This fact created tensions in both families. The problems, though, mainly fell on Mom's shoulders. It was customary for the wife to follow the husband's lead. Mom would now have to leave the synagogue of the Turkish Jews and become part of the Rhodes community, where she was a virtual stranger. She got a taste of the impact of this impending transition at her wedding. One of Dad's older relatives, a woman who had been born in Rhodes, made a point of introducing herself to my mother. In the course of her conversation, she referred to my mother as an ajena, a foreigner. (This was a term used by Jews of Rhodes to designate anyone not of Rhodes ancestry.) My mother promptly and uncharacteristically responded with anger. "I am no ajena; I was born right here in America. You are the ajena." The relative was undaunted. She smiled back at Mom with a haughty expression on her face.

Already at her wedding, she could foresee problems she would face as she adjusted to her new life. Holidays, formerly observed in her parents' home, would now be observed with her husband's family. All of her husband's relatives were now her relatives as well; in those days, relatives had claims on your hospitality and generosity. Mom would have to integrate a whole new set of people into her life.

If Mom and her parents cried at the wedding, at least some of the tears stemmed from the fear that their relationship would be hurt in the transition. On one level, my grandparents were gaining a son. But on another level, they feared they were losing a daughter.

As things ultimately turned out, Mom did her best to become part of my Dad's family. But her ties to her own family were so strong that she gradually succeeded in moving Dad into her family's orbit. Dad came to love Mom's parents. As the years passed, our family became part of the extended family of my Mom's parents. We were together with them on Sabbaths and holidays, we went on vacation together, we were at their home often. Mom's sisters and brothers and their children were at the center of our family's life.

So Mom, in her own quiet and steady way, had brought Dad into her family. She was most certainly not an ajena in her own family life and friendships.

After a short honeymoon, my parents moved into a small cold water flat at 20th and Alder. The following year, they moved into an apartment in a duplex owned by an elderly Sephardic couple, at 23rd and Cherry. Dad was earning $22.50 per week at his fruit stand in the Broadway Market. Although this was a good income in those days, he was still burdened by debts accrued during his illness and hospitalization the year before he and Mom were married.

Dad held the traditional attitude that a married woman should not work out of the home. It was the husband's role to provide for his wife and family. So Mom quit her job at the candy factory and started a new life as a homemaker. (She resented the term "housewife.")

Within a year, my brother Bill was born. Although he grew up to be a calm, soft-spoken gentleman, he was a noisy baby. He cried day and night. Mom used all her ingenuity to keep her new baby quiet and happy but Bill was not easily pacified. Dad brought home a book on how to raise children and insisted that Mom follow the advice faithfully. Mom would feed Bill according to the schedule listed in the book; she would put him to sleep at the times recommended in the book. But Bill continued to be a difficult baby.

On a visit to the pediatrician, Mom told the doctor of her troubles. Her patience was wearing thin; she was exhausted and frustrated. The doctor asked: "Are you following instructions from a book?"

"Yes, of course."

"Throw out the book," the doctor ordered. "Just follow your own common sense. Your baby is a human being like you. Are you hungry according to a schedule in a book? Are you sleepy every day at the exact same time? Why should the baby want to follow a schedule from a book?"

Mom broke out in a smile at this sensible advice. She felt much relieved. When Dad came home from work that night, Mom informed him of the doctor's instructions: throw out the book. Dad was not pleased with the doctor; only a quack would advise a parent to throw out such a famous book on child rearing. After another noisy week with Bill, Mom gathered the courage to actually toss out the book. Dad had no choice but to go along with the decision.

A problem arose with the landlord and his wife. They were elderly and they liked peace and tranquility. They did not like to hear crying babies. The landlord asked my parents to find another place to live and to find it quickly.

Dad, in one of his characteristic strokes of boldness, determined that it was time to buy a house rather than to rent another apartment. So the search for a house began.

To the extent that Dad was bold and determined, so Mom was nervous and afraid. How would they be able to pay for a house? Wasn't a house too great a responsibility for them at such a young age?

The two of them found time to visit homes that were for sale. Mom would examine each house from top to bottom, carefully noting every detail. In each instance, she found something wrong. One house was too large, another was too small. One needed too much work, one was too ostentatious. Some were too far from her parents' home on 15th Avenue. All were too expensive.

As the house search dragged on, the landlord was becoming more and more impatient. He wanted them to move out immediately. The more pressure he put on my parents, the more Mom stalled for time.

Dad, whose patience during this process was remarkable, explained to Mom that they really had no choice: they had to move as soon as possible. She could not expect to find a perfect house but she would have to settle for the best she could find. Mom finally accepted the inevitability of their moving, regardless of the expenses and risks involved.

One Sunday, a real estate man by the name of Mr. Bloomer called my parents and told them he had a house to show them. It was a nice house; but the owner was an eccentric and mean-spirited man. Sometimes he would allow prospective buyers into the house and sometimes he would not. The house had been for sale for a long time, but the owner managed to scare off all the potential buyers.

Mr. Bloomer drove my parents to the house—511 28th Avenue, between Jefferson and East Cherry. Mom looked at the house from the car. Spontaneously she said: "This is the house. We'll buy it."

Dad was even more surprised than Mr. Bloomer. He asked: "You haven't even seen the inside of the house. How can you be sure this is the one we should buy?"

Mom responded that she was sure. She fell in love with it on sight.

Meanwhile, Mr. Bloomer had gone up the front steps to ask the owner to let my parents take a look at the house. The owner was in one of his bad moods; he slammed the door and said no one would be allowed inside.

Mr. Bloomer discussed the situation with my parents. Mom's confidence was so overwhelming that Dad agreed to make an offer to purchase the house. Mr. Bloomer felt that the owner would take an offer of $2000. Dad told him that he would like to make the offer but that he did not have enough available money for a down payment. Amazingly, Mr. Bloomer told my parents that he himself would make the down payment, two hundred dollars; they could pay him back a little at a time.

And that is what happened. Mr. Bloomer made the down payment, my parents got a mortgage for the rest, and they made a schedule for repaying Mr. Bloomer for his interest-free loan. They bought the house without having seen the inside of it. In a short time, they moved in; Mom's love for the house only deepened when she first entered it. She had an almost mystical affection for it throughout the eighteen years (1940-1958) in which she lived in it. She was broken-hearted when we had to move to a new neighborhood, and never fully overcame her sense of loss at leaving it.

While my parents were busy buying and moving into 511 28th Avenue, the world was facing a war of massive proportions. The Germans had already established their nefarious concentration camps in which they murdered millions of people. Hitler's anti-Jewish propaganda and his incarceration of vast numbers of Jews sent shudders through the hearts of Jews throughout the world—including Seattle. While the European allies were quivering before the power of the Nazis, the American public was worrying whether our country would be drawn into the war. As millions of Jews were murdered in Nazi death camps, the United States pursued a policy of staying out of the fray. Moreover, the U.S. sealed its borders to all but a few refugees. The anti-immigrant mood directly resulted in the deaths of many thousands of victims of the Germans. They simply had nowhere to flee for safety; they were left to perish.

When Japan attacked Pearl Harbor, it became clear that the United States could not avoid war. The entire country was mobilized to fight the Japanese threat. The U.S. also sent troops to Europe to help the allies fight the Germans and their accomplices.

Patriotic fervor ran high in America. The Sephardic community of Seattle was no exception. Young men volunteered or were drafted into the military service. Dad was exempted since he was head of a family that was dependent on him for support. Moreover, his history of having had pneumonia and his chronic bronchial problems factored into the decision not to draft him.

My Uncle Vic, though, was drafted even though he, too, was the head of a family that depended on him. Being younger and in better health than my father, Uncle Vic was sent to the Far East where he served in battle. Due to his poor eyesight and his dependence on his glasses, he asked to be stationed in a position where his life would not be endangered if his glasses would be broken. He was sent to the front lines!

During his absence from Seattle, his wife Estreya (my mother's sister) moved into our home together with her baby daughter Esther Lee. The anxieties of war reverberated in 511 28th Avenue, as in so many American homes. Mom's role expanded as she became a matriarch and source of strength to her sister and baby niece.

Mom got together with a group of Sephardic women to help the American war effort. They formed a group under the umbrella of the American Red Cross, sewing and knitting garments for American soldiers stationed abroad. They worked long hours

and made numerous items. In order to underscore the seriousness of their efforts, they made themselves special uniforms and
established membership dues. At their early meetings, they struggled to find a suitable name for their group. My Uncle Dave suggested "Knit Wits," but the women, understandably, rejected it.
They finally settled on the name: "Sephardic Do-Our-Bit Club."
After the war, Mom and the other women in the club each received a certificate of merit from the American Red Cross that
included the stamped signature of President Truman.

In July 1944, the Jews of the Island of Rhodes were deported
to Auschwitz. Nearly every family of Congregation Ezra Bessaroth had relatives still living in Rhodes at the time. Communica-
tion between Rhodes and Seattle was all but non-existent during
the war years. As news of the deportation gradually reached
Seattle, a wave of despair and mourning swept the community.
Only after the war did our family learn that my father's brother
Joseph had died in 1943. His wife, Sinyoru, and their children—
Leon, Bulissa, Jacob and Sarah-- were among those deported to
and murdered in Auschwitz.

In July 1945, one year after the destruction of the Jewish community of Rhodes, my parents had a new baby. As indicated earlier, I was that baby.

Now that the war had ended with victory, a spirit of optimism
arose in America. Dad and his brother Ray opened a fruit stand
in the Broadway Market. Patriotically, they named it "Victory
Fruit Market."

Their entrepreneurship led them to soon start out on a new
business venture. They bought a number of pinball and shuf-
fleboard machines, as well as juke boxes, for which they leased
space in taverns. Customers paid to play games and listen to records; Dad and Uncle Ray would keep the profits. They were
busy day and night trying to lease spaces; checking up on the
machines that were in service; collecting the money; arranging
for the repair of machines that broke down. Moreover, they had
to spend much of their time in taverns. They sometimes got into
scuffles with men who had drunk more beer than they could
handle. Mom hated the business from the outset, urging Dad to

go back to his roots in the food business.

While Dad and Uncle Ray were in their new venture, we children enjoyed a fringe benefit. Every now and then, Dad would bring home a large box of 45 rpm records that had been almost completely worn out in the juke boxes. As far as we were concerned, they were still playable, and we played them with tremendous enjoyment. We were the envy of many friends and neighbors who were not so fortunate to have such a fabulous collection of popular records.

After a year or two in this business, Dad gave in to Mom and returned to his original occupation. He opened a grocery store at 621 Broadway East, and named it Angel's Food Center. He proudly stated that he always wanted to have his name in lights on Broadway…and now he succeeded in doing so! He found a partner—Al Israel—and they maintained the business until Dad's decision to retire in 1975.

Angel's Food Center flourished in spite of serious handicaps. It was too small to be called a supermarket; yet it was too large to be a little family store that could operate without employees. It had no parking lot. It had to compete with much larger supermarkets within the same vicinity. The odds were against my father making a success of this business.

But Dad did make his store into a success. He firmly believed that small businesses could thrive in America; that hard work is always rewarded. He could succeed by providing personal service, by greeting his regular customers by name, by delivering groceries to their homes, by taking orders by telephone. His remarkable sense of humor and his basic optimism won the affection and respect of his customers. He was constantly smiling, cracking jokes, making puns. He used to say: "The little guy can succeed in America if he works hard…and knows how to accept life with a good sense of humor."

Dad explained to me some of the secrets of his success. He insisted on selling only the best merchandise. His specialty was having the highest quality fruits and vegetables, and presenting them in an appealing display. He trained his employees to put out only the best produce, properly trimmed. Whatever was not aesthetically up to grade—he brought home for us!

I was once in the store when a woman came in and asked for a bottle of soda. I offered to run back and get it. Dad held me back, and told her the number of the aisle where the soda could be found. When she went to find the soda, Dad told me that it was best to let the customer go through the store when searching for a particular item. More often than not, he or she would find other items to purchase. And so it was. The woman came back with the soda...plus quite a few other groceries. "You have to understand psychology to be in business," Dad often would say.

He once had a customer who asked to buy a copy of yesterday's newspaper. Dad told him that he only had today's edition. The customer left. The next day, the same thing happened: the customer asked for yesterday's paper. Again Dad told him that he only had today's paper. The next day, the customer again came in with the same request. This time Dad gave him a copy of today's paper, told him to buy it and put it away in a drawer so he would have it for tomorrow morning. The customer liked this suggestion and bought the paper.

One of the ongoing problems of the grocery business is dealing with shoplifters. Dad had mirrors installed on the ceiling throughout the store and had signs posted to indicate that shoplifters would be prosecuted to the full extent of the law. These precautions did not deter everyone. Some shoppers would pick up a handful of cherries and eat them while they were doing their shopping. Others would open boxes of cookies or packages of candies and eat them on the spot. Generally, such people were caught and were told in a nice way that they had to pay for what they took. In the case of repeat offenders, Dad would tell them that they should do their shopping elsewhere.

On one occasion, a man attempted to steal a cantaloupe by putting it down the front of his shirt. Dad detected this crime in one of the store's mirrors. When the fellow came up to the check-out stand, Dad rang up the few items the criminal had brought to the counter. Then Dad rang up another charge of $10. The man asked what the extra $10 charge was for. Dad told him it was for the cantaloupe that he had dropped down the front of his shirt. The man did not blush or seem perturbed; rather, he immediately took the offensive. "Cantaloupes only cost one dollar, so why are you charging me ten dollars? That's not legal."

Dad replied calmly. "The price of a cantaloupe is one dollar if you bring it to the counter in a shopping cart. But if you bring a cantaloupe hidden in your shirt, the price is ten dollars." The man threatened to call the police. Dad handed him the telephone. Flustered and angry, the man paid for his groceries including the ten dollar surcharge. Dad told him to do his shopping in the future at the big supermarket a few blocks away.

Angel's Food Center had four large rolling stands on which fruits and berries would be displayed. The stands were rolled out onto the sidewalk in front of the store. By-passers would be attracted to the items and would often buy some. This was a very successful aspect of the business, especially during the summer months.

The big supermarkets nearby, that did vastly more business than Angel's Food Center, nevertheless did their best to destroy Dad's business. A manager of one of these supermarkets called the police and insisted that Dad be fined for putting displays on the sidewalk, in public space. When the policeman gave Dad a summons, Dad was stupefied. He had been placing these stands on the sidewalk for years. They were pushed up right against the store. They bothered no one, nor did they interfere in any way with pedestrian traffic. Many other stores did the same thing. The police officer was apologetic, but he issued the summons. Dad was forced to have the stands rolled back into the store so that no part of them rested on the sidewalk. Some of his optimism about American business faded on that day. He was outraged that the big supermarkets didn't want 90% of the trade; they wanted all of it. As long as Dad lived, he never could understand that attitude. And as long as he lived, he never became a wealthy man.

The big supermarkets tried other strategies to undermine Angel's Food Center. They began to open seven days a week, 24 hours a day. How could a small grocery store compete? It was impossible and impractical for Dad's store to stay open at all times.

One day, someone from the Teamsters union came to the store and told Dad that he had to join the union. Since the store had a delivery truck, he was obligated to pay the Teamsters. Dad did not wish to join the union and didn't see why he should. The union sent a group of noisy picketers in front of Angel's Food Center, scaring customers away. After holding out about a week, Dad joined the union. He saw this as paying protection money.

Some years after Dad had joined the Teamsters, a union representative showed up at the store and told Dad that he was no longer eligible to be a member of the union. Dad was very pleased to learn this news. He came home from work that night with a broad smile on his face.

"Once in a while, the little guy gets a break in America," he quipped. "Usually it's a break of the head, but once in a while it's a real break."

Dad never became a wealthy man, but he lived as though he were rich. He subscribed to the philosophy that wealth is what you spend. What you have in the bank is only potential wealth.

We always lived nicely. We had a nice home, a nice car, and nice clothes. Although we lived relatively simply, we did not feel that we were deprived. We had an idea of our financial limits and we lived comfortably within the boundaries.

My parents' sense of pride demanded that we live at a proper economic level, without going into debt. Mom was especially eager that we not appear to be poor.

Mom's pride caused me some discomfort as a child. Most of my school friends had "taps"—metal strips—attached to the soles and heels of their shoes. The taps were meant to preserve the bottom of the shoes so that the soles and heels would not wear out. This, of course, saved money. But children did not wear taps because of the economic concern, but because taps were fun. They made neat sounds. They clicked on the floors of the halls in school. They made grinding noises on the concrete playground.

I also wanted to have taps put on my shoes. Mom was adamantly opposed: "Poor people wear taps." I explained to her that taps were fun, that all the children had them. Mom responded: "You will not have taps on your shoes. Taps are for poor people."

That ended the matter.

Mom had a similar attitude about jeans. Jeans were sturdy and rugged. They were fashionable among my friends. Cowboys wore them, so what could be wrong with jeans?

Mom generally got me corduroy pants. I liked them but I also wanted jeans. Mom told me pointedly: "Poor people wear jeans." I reminded her that cowboys wore jeans and cowboys weren't poor. Mom was not impressed with my argument. "You are not a cowboy, you are not going to wear jeans."

On my twelfth birthday, one of my uncles bought me a pair of jeans for a present. This was a special pair that had reinforced knees so it could endure a lot of wear and tear. I was delighted. Mom was not.

After several days of my nagging her, she finally gave in. Mom said I could wear them, but only on Sundays for playing outside. I was not allowed to wear them to school. I remember my glee when first putting on the new jeans. As things turned out, I managed to wear holes into them in a relatively short period of time in spite of the reinforced knees. As soon as I did, Mom gave the jeans to an organization that collected clothes for poor people.

This brings us to another of Mom's policies: we could not

wear clothes that had been repaired with patches. Mom sewed quite well. She repaired torn garments and made them look like new. But if any tear was so bad as to require a patch, the garment was given away or converted into canimazos, rags. Why? "Poor people wear clothes with patches."

Mom had nothing against poor people. She had known first-hand what it meant to be poor. She simply did not want poverty or the stigma of poverty to hang over her family. Taps, jeans and patches were symbols of a station in life that she was trying to move beyond.

Dad shared the same attitude. It manifested itself, for example, in the cars he bought. He did not believe in buying used cars. Used cars were for people who could not afford better or who were too tight with their money to buy a new car. Dad did not look down on those who bought used cars; but he would not buy one himself.

The first car I remember was our 1950 Buick Roadmaster. It was a two-tone blue, four door sedan that was built like a tank. The car cost $3000—this was $1000 more than our house had cost only ten years earlier.

Dad named the car "Old Faithful" and it lived up to its name. It gave six years of excellent service. It was a symbol of Dad's success.

"Old Faithful" was a unique vehicle among our extended family. It was new, expensive, and fashionable—and it worked. Most of our relatives had cars of a different genre: used, inexpensive, downscale and temperamental.

Uncle Jack had a jalopy that he named "Geraldine." He used to park the car on the top of hills, with the car facing downhill. The reason for this strategy was that Geraldine did not always start when the ignition was turned on. When this occurred, as I myself witnessed on various occasions, he would have someone push the car from behind so that it started rolling down the hill. Once the car was rolling, Uncle Jack would turn on the ignition and floor the gas pedal. This usually got the car started.

Uncle Solomon had a car of comparable character. I remember a Friday afternoon when he called to offer me a ride to synagogue. He told me to meet him at his house on 26th Avenue. I was glad for the ride, since I usually would walk the mile or so to synagogue. When I arrived, I found my uncle and several of my cousins waiting for me. We got into the car, but Uncle Solomon could not get the automobile to start. He asked us to get out and push the car until the ignition caught. We pushed the car for several blocks but its motor remained silent. We asked my uncle what we should do. He answered: keep pushing. And we did. We ended up pushing the car all the way to the synagogue without its engine ever having started. We pushed it to the top of a hill a block away from the synagogue where Uncle Solomon parked it before Shabbat.

On Saturday night, he offered us a ride home, and we were foolish enough to accept. We pushed the car out of its parking spot and watched it roll down the hill. The ignition did not catch. We ended up pushing the car all the way home.

We deserved it.

After a few years with our two-tone blue Old Faithful, Mom thought the car needed to be refinished. Dad obliged and had the car colors changed: gray on top, white on the bottom. With its fresh look, the car seemed to be new again.

In 1956, Dad decided it was time for a new car. He bought a Chevrolet, with a cream color top and a red body. This car he also named "Old Faithful" and it, too, provided years of good service. Future "Old Faithfuls" were purchased in 1962, 1972 and 1981. In all cases, Dad followed his basic philosophy in buying cars: the cars had to be new, American made, good looking and comfortable.

We were not only in the forefront of our extended family when it came to cars; we also were leaders when it came to home entertainment machines. Before the introduction of television, we had a fashionable mahogany console. On one side was a radio and on the other side was a phonograph. This impressive piece of furniture and modern technology was at the vanguard of fashion in those years. Relatives and friends would come to our house to enjoy the radio and to hear the records on the phonograph.

When televisions came out, our console was destined to become obsolete. Everyone wanted to watch T.V. However, since televisions were quite expensive, not everyone could afford to buy one.

The first ones in our extended family to have a television set were Uncle Solomon and Aunty Sarah (my mother's sister). They had entered a raffle and were the lucky ones to win a new T.V. It only had a ten inch screen, surrounded by a huge light brown console. A rabbit ear antenna sat atop it.

The first time I saw television was at Uncle Solomon and Aunty Sarah's house. Shortly after they had received the television, they invited dozens of family members to come to their home to watch programs on this amazing new invention. We arrived with a great sense of anticipation.

Uncle Solomon had perched the television console on a high case in the living room, and had set up rows of folding chairs for the audience. Aunty Sarah made a huge batch of popcorn. As we excitedly found seats and chatted about the wonders of modern technology, Uncle Solomon called for silence. With a great dramatic flair, he turned the set on.

All of us strained to get a good view of the ten inch screen. We saw some light, then some darkness, sounds of static. Black lines flashed across the screen. Soon, the T.V. warmed up and a picture appeared on the screen. It was very blurry. Uncle Solomon fiddled with the antenna ears until the picture cleared up a bit. The sound was gravelly, the picture was jumbled. In spite of these factors, we watched the program in awe. It was as though we were witnessing an incredible miracle.

When the program ended, Uncle Solomon proudly went to the front of the room and turned off the set. We were clapping with delight. We had entered a new era.

After that sensational evening, Dad decided that our family ought to have a television too. Within a short time, he ordered a Sylvania with a sixteen inch screen. To ensure good reception, we had an antenna attached to the roof of our house. We did not have the first television set in the family, but for the moment we certainly had the most impressive.

My parents' philosophy was to buy the best item one could afford. Owning nice things gives a sense of pride and pleasure. Moreover, it is practical: good quality merchandise lasts longer and works better.

Dad was a stickler for paying bills on time. When he had to make mortgage payments on our house, he made advance payments as frequently as he could in order to retire the debt at the soonest possible moment. He considered it a matter of personal pride that his credit was excellent, that he was a respectable and honorable businessman. When expenses posed problems for him, he found creative ways to deal with them.

For example, our family's teeth were cared for by an excellent—and very expensive—dentist. Dad was loyal to this dentist because they had grown up together as children and had lived across the street from one another. As long as the dentist did not have to do too much work on our teeth, Dad managed to pay the bills without any trouble. Often enough, though, we needed fillings or other expensive work. In those cases, the bills came to a considerable amount, more than Dad could pay at one time. On the other hand, Dad could not rest when he owed money, feeling that it was a disgrace to be in debt. How could he pay the dentist's bills if he did not have enough money available?

Dad came up with a solution: he paid with groceries. The dentist bought groceries at Angel's Food Center. The amount of the groceries was deducted from the amount owed for his dental services. The old-fashioned barter system worked, and the two of them got along fine.

Dad had a notion that a properly brought up young lady must know how to play the piano. He arranged for my sister to take piano lessons with a teacher who lived not far from his store. Usually, he had no problem paying for the lessons; but when he was under extreme financial pressure, he paid with groceries. This was a fair exchange: food for culture.

My parents both stressed the importance of having a good reputation-- being honest, decent, generous and imbued with self-respect. It also meant being true to yourself, not pretending to be what you were not. Mom used to tell me: "Always try your best. It is no shame to fail; it is a shame to give up, to lie, to cheat, to be dishonest." And she would add: "Be good at whatever you do. If you are going to be a bum, be a good bum!"

Mom and Dad believed in living according to one's means. On the one hand, this entailed not going into debt to buy things beyond one's economic level. On the other hand, it meant not living at a lower level than one could afford. They had little sympathy for nouveaux riches types or for people who were meticulously frugal.

Dad always bought nice cars, but not "luxury" cars. Mom always wore a nice coat, but not a mink coat. They found a good balance between being comfortable and maintaining simplicity.

Mom lauded the greatness of the simple, working people whom she called "the salt of the earth." She quoted the Judeo-Spanish proverb, el rey es con la gente, the king is with the people. True nobility of character demanded a close relationship with the common folk. One who stands aloof from or looks down on the working classes is not only a snob but is ignoble. Along with all our relatives, my parents voted for Democrats, believing that the Democrats stood for the working classes.

In the 1952 presidential campaign, the candidates were General Dwight David Eisenhower for the Republicans and Adlai Stevenson for the Democrats. I asked Mom if she was going to vote for Eisenhower, since she had named me after him. She responded: "General Eisenhower is a great man. But I'm voting for Stevenson, the Democrat."

I was only seven years old at the time and I felt insulted that she would vote against the man whose name she had given me. Seeing my consternation, she re-assured me that Eisenhower was a wonderful general and fine person. However, he had been brainwashed to become a Republican. The Republicans looked out mainly for the rich. Only the Democrats cared about the working people. Adlai Stevenson was the Democratic candidate, so he was on our side.

I was still not assuaged.

At school, our teacher assigned us to make a campaign poster either for Eisenhower or Stevenson. My instincts were all for Eisenhower. I started on several posters for Ike, but made various mistakes leading me to discard them. I liked Ike but I was having trouble making a poster in his support. So I decided to make a Stevenson poster. Everything fell into place easily. I concluded that I, too, must really have been for the Democrats.

I brought the poster home to show Mom. She was so pleased with it that she mailed it to the Stevenson campaign headquarters. Some weeks later, I received a letter from the Stevenson committee thanking me for my support. Mom put the letter on the mantle in the living room. It was a proud moment for us.

Although I was glad to be identified with the Stevenson campaign, in my heart of hearts I still felt a tugging toward Dwight Eisenhower, my namesake. When the election results came in and Eisenhower was declared the victor, my parents were downcast. I offered them some consolation: "At least we have a President named Dwight!"

"Yes," Mom responded, "and he is a great man even if he is a Republican."

Part IV

Transitions of The Next Generation

I grew up as part of an extended family that had a clear sense of the role of each member. The men were the breadwinners. They worked to support the women and children. In return for their labor, the men were considered to be the head of their families and were accorded certain privileges.

In our family, for example, Dad had his own place at the head of the table. He had his own place on the living room couch. Neither my mother nor any of the children would sit in his place. Likewise, although we were free to express our opinions, Dad's opinion was authoritative. In fact, he often deferred to Mom's opinion. Even then, Mom would make it appear that the decision had really been Dad's.

Women were expected to care for the family and the home. In our extended family, the women were excellent cooks. They kept their homes in good order and taught their children proper manners. In return, they also were entitled to respect. Mom had her own honored place at the table as well as her own designated armchair in the living room.

Mom had a rule: the children could not ask Dad any questions nor make any requests of him until he first finished eating his dinner. He put in long hours at the store, usually not arriving home until after 9:30 pm. He would be exhausted and hungry.

We developed a routine. When Dad drove the car (or sometimes the truck from the store) up the driveway, he would honk the horn a few times. The older children would run out to greet him and would carry in the groceries he had brought home. He entered the house where he was greeted warmly by Mom. He then would wash up and come to the dinner table. By the time he sat down, Mom had already put his hot dinner at his place. She would overload the plate with meat and a variety of side dishes and would also have a salad of lettuce and tomatoes ready for him.

When we were very young, we often were sleeping before Dad got home. As we grew older, we were allowed the privilege of sitting down with him when he ate his dinner. He ate with such gusto that we would become hungry, even though we had eaten dinner earlier. More often than not, Mom would end up feeding us again "to keep Dad company." Although she also ate dinner earlier, she would fix herself a plate with a few things so she could eat something with Dad. She did not think it was proper to let him eat alone.

Mom prepared elaborate meals every night. She cooked the traditional foods of the Turkish and Rhodes Jews, many of which required considerable preparation. Dad did not consider it dinner if he did not have meat. Fish meals, thus, were ruled out. If Mom wanted to make fish, it could only be served before the "real" dinner. Dad also did not consider a vegetarian or dairy meal to be dinner. Chinese food also did not count. Mom accepted these basic premises and cooked accordingly. Her philosophy was simple: her husband worked hard all day, so he was entitled to a good dinner that would satisfy him.

After Dad had eaten his dinner, we would have time for our family conversations. He would tell us about the various happenings of the day at his store; we would tell him of our activities. The length of the conversation would be determined by the degree of Dad's tiredness or his patience.

We learned from Mom that Dad deserved all the respect we could give him in light of his overwhelming sacrifices on our behalf. When he was thirsty, one of us children would run to bring him a glass of water with ice cubes—his most refreshing drink. When he sat down in the living room, one of us would bring him pillows or a footrest to make him more comfortable.

Dad enjoyed telling jokes and making puns. Each Friday, one of the children would be responsible for going down the block to Sam's Drugstore to buy two comic books. Dad preferred comics such as Archie, Dagwood and Blondie, Sad Sack, and Beatle Baily. Since he took the day off on Saturday in observance of the Sabbath, he enjoyed reading the comics on Shabbat afternoons. He would invariably read some of the jokes to us and we would laugh together uncontrollably. Dad was especially jovial on the Sabbaths, when he was more relaxed, and when he had a captive audience with his family. When he would tell a joke on Friday night, Mom would announce: "Shabbat is officially here!"

Not only were we taught to respect our parents, we also learned to show honor to all elders. We were not to look elders directly in the eye. Rather, the eyes should be aimed downward as a sign of respect. To look an elder in the eye was brazen; it was as if to imply that we were the equal of the elder—which of course we were not.

This particular mannerism eventually caused me some difficulty later in life. When I first began serving my congregation, I was a twenty-four year old rabbinical student. I was, naturally, eager to succeed in my position. It is customary to have a gathering following Sabbath morning services at which Kiddush is recited, refreshments are served, and congregants socialize with each other. In following the pattern of the senior clergy, I used this opportunity to chat with congregants.

One of the elder ladies of the congregation, a woman of great influence in the community, called the president of the congregation to complain about me. She said I was aloof and cold, not at all friendly. When the president conveyed these criticisms to me, I was surprised. I had greeted this woman warmly and enthusiastically when I had seen her on Shabbat.

The following Shabbat, I made a special point of paying my respects to her. But the next day, I received another call from the president in which he once again repeated the woman's criticisms. I assured him that I had been friendly and respectful to her, but he told me to try harder!

In discussing this problem with my wife, she asked me if I looked the woman in the eye when I spoke with her. "Of course not," I replied. Gilda then advised: "This Shabbat, look her straight in the eye when you greet her." I was jolted. "That would be rude on my part. She would become even more hostile to me." Gilda insisted that I follow her advice.

The next Shabbat morning after services, I went over to the woman, looked her right in the eye, and wished her a good Sabbath. I felt discomfited by this show of arrogance on my part.

The next day, the president called me. "She loves you," he said. "She is so pleased that you are friendly and sociable after all."

I still did not understand how to interpret this strange episode. Gilda clarified the matter for me. I was raised to think that it was disrespectful to look an elder in the eye. However, American culture generally teaches that it is disrespectful not to look someone in the eye. A lack of eye contact implies a lack of interest and concern. What I had considered a gesture of respect, the elderly congregant had taken as a sign of disinterest and aloofness.

I learned an important life lesson. If people do not understand each other's cultural signals, they might very well misinterpret those signals and thereby come into conflict. I also learned the importance of looking others in the eye when speaking with them!

Another thing we learned as children was not to ask for seconds of food when we were guests in anyone's home. No matter how hungry we still felt and no matter how much we desired a particular item of food, we could not ask for seconds. If the hostess offered seconds, we were obliged to decline. If she asked again and was insistent, then we could take seconds. In fact, if the hostess insisted on giving us seconds, then we had to accept even if we did not like or want the food. To reject her hospitality would be an insult.

In our community, children learned to kiss the hand of parents and grandparents in order to receive a blessing. This was generally done on Friday nights, but it was also practiced on holidays and other special occasions. I remember when my grandfather Romey would be called to the Torah during Sabbath morning services, all of his children, grandchildren and younger relatives would stand in his honor. When he returned to his seat, we would form a line in order of age, and we would kiss his hand and receive his blessing.

In those days, the family had a definite structure. Respect for elders was deeply inculcated in the young. Good manners were required. Those days were not without problems; but life had a clear context and meaning.

The Talmud instructs: do not disdain anything, for everything has its place. It also teaches that it is a sin to be wasteful. In short, things have value and should be respected.

In our family, we learned the value of things in various ways. Before eating, we were taught to recite the appropriate blessing to thank God for our food. Papoo would say the blessing over bread and then would kiss the loaf before cutting it into pieces and distributing it to the family. It was considered a sin to throw bread or even to let it drop to the floor.

Leftover food was not thrown away. Nona had taught her daughters how to "recycle" leftovers, turning them into healthy and tasty meals. Leftover chicken and vegetables would become chicken pot pie or stew; or they could become the basis of a hearty soup. Leftover baked goods would become toast, stuffing, or crunchy snacks known as parmakes. Stale bread was soaked in water and then squeezed. Eggs and cheese were mixed into the bread pulp, and patties were formed from this mixture. They were fried until brown on both sides and were a special treat known as boyos de pan. When there were too many vegetables at home and there was a fear that they would begin to rot, we would have a meal called quartos, fourths; this was a stew made by cutting all the vegetables into quarters and simmering them in a pot. Ripening fruit would become homemade jam. When there was no way to save the food for human consumption, it was fed to the neighbors' dogs. Inedible bread was fed to the ducks along the shore of Lake Washington.

Delicious side dishes were made from celery roots (apyo), spinach stems (ravicos), and zucchini peels (cashcaricas). Coffee grounds and onion skins were placed in the water in which hard boiled eggs were cooked. The egg shells turned brown, and the flavors were absorbed by the eggs themselves. Known as huevos haminados, these eggs were a specialty for Sabbath and festival meals.

Orange peels could be made into candy or added to baked goods for flavoring. Nona would sometimes place pieces of orange peel and cloves on the burners of her stove in order to give the house a nice fragrance. When Mom peeled apples for baking pies, we would eat the apple peels as a snack.

This heartfelt concern for food was symbolic of a philosophy of life that valued things. Indeed, a society might be evaluated by its garbage. If it discards edible and usable things, it is extravagant. A wasteful society shows disrespect for God's blessings. Long before environmentalism and conservation became fashionable, our culture fostered a deep and abiding connection with the natural resources we enjoyed.

Clothes were kept until they were worn out. If they were outgrown but still wearable, they were given to another family member who could use them. For years, I wore shirts handed down to me from my older brother Bill. For years, my younger brother David wore hand me downs from me. If no one in our immediate family needed or wanted the used clothes, Mom would have the clothing picked up by an agency that provided clothes for the poor.

Without realizing it, our extended family was avant garde when it came to recycling. We used juice bottles as vases for flowers. Jars from peanut butter and jam were used as drinking glasses; or as containers for buttons and sundry items. Cardboard boxes were used as storage bins, receptacles for the family photographs, even as luggage. When we went on vacation, we packed cardboard boxes with pots and pans, meat, bread and other kosher groceries that we would not be able to find at our vacation destination.

And of course we had collections.

We collected rocks, sea shells, sand dollars, sticks, bottle caps, baseball cards, books, knick-knacks, marbles, coins, stamps, jack-knives. None of our collections was scientific; all were spontaneous and fun, without a thought as to future value.

Some of the things we collected had practical uses. For example, we would go to a beach at Deception Pass at the northern tip of Whidbey Island in search of "cheese rocks." Mom used to make white cheese *(queso blanco)*, similar to farmer's cheese. Part of the process required putting the curdling milk into cheesecloth and placing it in a pan. For the cheese to solidify, it was necessary for the watery part of the milk to drain. This was accomplished by placing a "cheese rock" on top of the cheesecloth. Mom liked "cheese rocks" that were oval, heavy and thick, and about six to eight inches long. A good "cheese rock" was a prize.

My jack-knife collection should also, at least theoretically, belong in the category of "useful" collections. I was careful to buy or trade for jack-knives that had a "personality." I did not like the plain ones that only had one or two blades. Generally, I bought my jack-knives at Mr. Schain's dry goods store on Yesler, between 23rd and 24th Avenues. I favored those with marbleized handles and that had an assortment of attachments. Among the features on my various knives were corkscrews, a screwdriver, scissors, an ice pick, a bottle opener—and of course blades of different sizes. Why did I buy these knives? I thought they were beautiful, strong and useful.

I cannot remember ever making use of them except to sharpen sticks that I never needed. One time I thought I could be helpful to Mom by using a jack-knife to open up a tightly closed pistachio nut. The result of my valor was that I sliced through the top of my thumb; I still have a scar to this day.

Although I was insistent on choosing knives that had cork-screw attachments, we never had bottles with corks that required use of a corkscrew. All the other attachments were equally un-necessary to me; or they simply did not work when they were needed. And still, I continued to collect jack-knives.

I learned that sometimes we collect things for the joy of col-lecting, not because we think the collectibles are really useful or valuable. If we enjoy collecting, that is sufficient reason to be a collector.

Mom was an avid collector of agates that we would find on the beach at Birch Bay, a resort in Northwest Washington State, a few miles from the Canadian border. Whenever we brought a rock to her for inspection, she would inform us if it was a real agate, or a partial agate, or just a plain rock. She liked small, white stones that you could almost see through when they were wet and you held them up to the sun. Mom also liked snail shells, but only if they were unbroken, and only if there were no live snails still inside them. Scouring the beach for agates and snail shells required considerable patience and concentration. It is a wonder that we children enjoyed this activity so much, since it was so time-consuming and meticulous. We never failed to leave Birch Bay without a cardboard box full of rocks and seashells. We generally also found some fine pieces of driftwood to add to the bounty that we brought back with us to Seattle.

What did we do with all those rocks, shells and sticks? Some of the rocks found a home in our goldfish bowl. Some of the more unusual pieces of driftwood ornamented the patio or garage. The rest stayed in boxes until somehow they just disappeared. The main fun and excitement had been in the finding and collecting.

One of the characteristic features of the homes in our ex-tended family was the display of halintrankas, dust catchers. This included all sorts of knick-knacks—glass fish, little statuettes, salt and pepper shakers etc. They generally were placed on the window sills in the kitchen. Where did these halintrankas come from? What purpose did they serve?

Most of them were won by us children as prizes when playing carnival games at Birch Bay. We would throw darts at balloons or at a moving disc with numbers on it; we would throw baseballs at bowling pins; we would throw dimes onto a table with numbers painted inside circles. Depending on how lucky we were, we won prizes. Generally, the prizes were fairly worthless halintrankas that no reasonable person would ever want or need. On the other hand, since we won the prizes, we were very proud of them.

Needless to say, these prizes could not be cast away. Rather, they had to be displayed proudly. The luckier we children were, the more halintrankas had to be accommodated in our homes. Whenever we won, we never failed to bring some of our best prizes to our grandparents so that they too could share in the joy.

After Nona died in 1959, Papoo kept the halintrankas in their places of honor on the kitchen window sills. When he died several years later, it became necessary to sell the house and dispose of the furnishings. I remember visiting the house for the last time. Everything was in turmoil. Mom and her siblings were going through the rooms, deciding who should take what; and what should be given away or sold. I drifted into the kitchen and my eyes fixed on the rows of halintrankas, covered with a thin layer of dust. They were so many useless things that had given so much pleasure over the years. There was a direct correlation between my grandparents' pleasure in them and our pleasure in them. Once my grandparents were gone, the halintrankas became ghosts of satisfactions long past. I asked Mom to take one of the halintrankas home as a memento. She did. I do not know what happened to the rest of them. It does not matter anymore.

Another category of collectibles were things that had no claim to intrinsic value but that stimulated our imagination. Whenever we received letters from abroad (not too often), we would cut the stamps off the envelopes and keep them in a cigar box. There was a certain awe that went with holding a stamp that had come from a faraway land. In some mysterious way, the stamp connected us with foreign civilizations. Each stamp, whether from Israel, Spain, Turkey or elsewhere, was received with enthusiasm.

Baseball cards also opened new worlds for us. Each card was not only a history of a particular player; it was also a window into another world, the world of major league baseball. In those days, players were loyal to their teams. A Yankee was a Yankee; a Dodger was a Dodger. Teams held together. Rapport developed between fans and the team for which they rooted. Trades, certainly involving the elite players, were not too common. As a little boy growing up in Seattle, where we only had a Triple A team back then, baseball cards symbolized a bigger world, a world where greatness could be achieved. Through the cards, we became part of greater America.

I collected things that had no apparent value or purpose at all. They were not useful, nor beautiful, nor did they stimulate imagination. In this category, I refer to my collection of bottle caps.

I do not remember why I started this collection. Somewhere around the time when I was nine years old, I was well into this project. I kept each type of bottle cap in a separate cigar box. Since Dad drank beer and we drank soft drinks fairly often, I was able to add a steady stream of caps to my collection. To get bottle caps from a wider variety of sources, I searched on sidewalks, beaches, neighbors' yards, or anywhere else I suspected I might find something to add to my collection. It was easy enough to obtain caps from Coca Cola, Seven Up, Budweiser and other popular brands. It was more difficult to find caps from foreign made beers and from less popular soft drinks. However, my collection was developing nicely, cap by cap.

One day I happened to mention my collection to my Uncle Dave Amon, a bartender at a tavern by the waterfront in downtown Seattle. His eyes brightened. "Do you like bottle caps?" he asked in wonderment. I proceeded to show him my cigar boxes containing the bottle caps I had collected.

Within a few days, Uncle Dave appeared at our back door with five or six bushel baskets of bottle caps. With glee and pride, he turned over this prize to me, patting me lovingly on the head. "In the tavern, we get an endless amount of bottle caps. I had all of them put into baskets for you. Now you have a really fantastic collection. And I'll keep bringing you lots more."

I hugged my uncle and thanked him. Together, we lugged the baskets down to the basement where I kept my collection. "Go ahead," he laughed once we had the baskets downstairs, "start sorting them out. You'll have a great time."

I started going through the baskets and fingering the caps, but somehow I felt a lack of enthusiasm and interest. My uncle had to leave fairly soon to get back to work. As he left, he assured me he'd be bringing me many more baskets of bottle caps in the weeks ahead.

From the moment I received this generous gift of many hundreds of bottle caps, I lost interest in my collection. I never bothered to sort through the baskets, I never placed the caps in their proper cigar boxes, and I stopped saving bottle caps from our dinner table. I scoured no more streets, yards or beaches.

When my uncle brought me another huge shipment of caps, I again thanked him…but without enthusiasm. He wasn't insulted, but he didn't seem pleased with my tepid response. After another few deliveries, he finally gave up on me. I thanked him profusely and told him that I already had all the bottle caps I would ever want and that I was no longer collecting them.

I later realized that the reason I had been collecting bottle caps was because it was fun to find things and categorize them. The rarer they were, the more challenging it was to find them, and the more thrilling to add them to the collection. Once the joy of collecting was removed due to the overabundant supply of bottle caps, the collection lost its meaning. It wasn't owning the collection that was important; it was the process of collecting.

Mom noticed my sudden abandonment of my bottle cap collection. She told me that collecting things provided a good lesson in life. Happiness is often found in the process of seeking a goal rather than in achieving it. Searching is more rewarding than finding. Self-reliance is more fulfilling than receiving gifts from others. We appreciate those things that have cost us time and effort more than things that have been given to us.

My bottle cap collection apparently had not been useless after all. It provided me with more useful insights than I had learned from many teachers and books.

French historian, Fernand Braudel, observed that "the mere smell of cooking can evoke a whole civilization." The aromas of foods contain within them the power to draw us back to the kitchens of our grandmothers, mother and aunties. We inhale the fragrance of freshly baked bread and we are children again.

The women in our family were excellent cooks, each expert in the cuisine of the Sephardic Jews of the Turkey and Rhodes. Although the American influence was apparent in our meals, the basic Mediterranean Sephardic cooking style prevailed.

Styles of food preparation separated one group from another. Mom told us that during her childhood years, palpable tensions would arise between the Sephardim and Ashkenazim of Seattle. One of the ways in which this rivalry manifested itself related to food. Ashkenazic youngsters would taunt their Sephardic peers by calling them "Mazola," since Sephardim traditionally cooked with vegetable oil such as Mazola brand oil. As a retort, the Sephardim called the Ashkenazim "schmaltz," the Yiddish word for chicken fat, a staple in Ashkenazic cooking.

It has long been a source of annoyance to Sephardim that Ashkenazim assume that their cooking is traditional Jewish cuisine, while that of the Sephardim falls into the category of exotica. It has been fairly common for people to write "Jewish" cookbooks that feature only Ashkenazic recipes; and write articles on "Jewish" cooking that ignored or misrepresented Sephardic cuisine. As a child attending the Jewish Day School in Seattle, I was taught that Jews eat latkes on Hanukkah and hamentaschen on Purim; yet, in our homes these foods were unknown. We ate bourmuelos on Hanukkah and foulares for Purim.

I vividly recall the first Shabbat I spent in the dormitory as a freshman at Yeshiva College in New York. After Friday evening services, we went to the cafeteria for dinner. At each place was a plate with a little brown round glob. I asked a classmate what this item was. He looked at me in disbelief. "Aren't you Jewish?" he asked me. Seeing my consternation, he finally told me that this glob was chopped liver, a dish eaten in honor of Shabbat. I had never seen, let alone eaten, chopped liver in my life. I went through the same culture shock that Shabbat when being served gefilte fish, matzah ball soup, cholent and kugel. While all of these foods were standard fare for Ashkenazim, they were entirely new to me. My classmates were stunned that I had been raised in such a "non-Jewish" fashion as not to have eaten these foods each Sabbath. While I learned to eat and enjoy most of the Ashkenazic foods, I have never completely gotten over the original pain I felt at the scorn of my classmates. They defined Jewishness according to their own pattern, without considering that there were other valid, traditional and vibrant patterns among other groups of Jews.

One of the main differences I found between the standard Ashkenazic and Sephardic cuisines relates to appearance. A plate of Ashkenazic food is typically brown, beige and orange. To dress up the color, sometimes they toss on a sprig of parsley. In contrast, a plate of Sephardic food is typically colorful and full of variety. Ashkenazim were big on potatoes, carrots and pasta. Sephardim, while also using these ingredients, drew on a wide repertoire of vegetables stemming from their Mediterranean cooking traditions.

When my wife, Gilda, first came to Seattle for our engagement, Passover 1967, she was amazed by the incredible variety of foods that she was served. Having been raised in an Ashkenazic home where the cuisine was brown and where vegetables came from cans, she was delighted to discover a whole new world of cooking. She was so pleased that she eventually went on to become an extraordinary cook and an author of a marvelous Sephardic cookbook, Sephardic Holiday Cooking.

As a child, I could tell what holiday was approaching by knowing what foods were being prepared. Before Rosh haShanah, Dad would bring home a large quantity of leeks, from which Mom would make leek patties (keftes de prasa). These were served as part of a pre-dinner ceremonial on the two nights of Rosh haShanah. Various foods were eaten on these occasions, each of which was symbolic of a good blessing for the New Year. Mom would make pumpkin-filled pastries; pastries with a filling that included beetroots; black-eyed beans cooked in a light tomato sauce. Uncooked symbolic foods included apples dipped in honey, dates and pomegranates.

On Succoth, we ate foods made with the autumn vegetables e.g. pumpkin, squash, zucchini, and leek. On Hanukkah we ate bourmuelos, deep fried doughnuts dipped in honey or powdered sugar. The fifteenth day of the Hebrew month of Shevat is known as the "New Year of Trees;" it is traditional to eat fruits, especially those grown in the land of Israel. A specialty of this holiday, known among us as fruticas, was a sweet pudding made from cracked wheat (prehito or mustrahana). In celebration of Purim, we ate foulares, a pastry made of a flat piece of dough with a hard-boiled egg wrapped in strips of dough. It looked vaguely like a foot—the flat dough being the foot, the egg being the ankle. It reminded us of the villain of the Purim story, Haman, who was defeated by Mordecai and Esther. Haman was hanged as punishment, possibly from his ankles.

Passover featured a vast assortment of foods made without bread or any leavened dough. We had special Passover bourmuelos, deep fried delicacies made of crushed matzah and egg; fritadas, a sort of quiche made of spinach and matzah; reshas fritas, strips of matzah soaked in egg and fried, and then eaten sprinkled with honey, sugar or jam. For breakfast, we broke matzah into little pieces and added sugar and milk. For drinks, we had shurup, which is made by mixing several spoonfuls of jam into a glass of cold water. On Shavuot we had foods featuring the available spring fruits and vegetables.

Each Sabbath was an occasion for festive meals. Mom used to

begin cooking on Thursday night and would be in the kitchen all day Friday. When we came home from school on Friday afternoons, we would find the kitchen counters loaded with things my mother had cooked: boulemas (yeast-dough pastries with various fillings such as spinach, potato, eggplant and cheese); bourekas, (pie-dough pastries, usually filled with a mixture of spinach or eggplant and cheese); pitas (round, flat cheese breads); soutlach (a pudding made of rice flour); panizicos (sweet rolls). Mom would also make cakes, pies, cookies, rice pudding and other sweets for the Shabbat meals.

I well remember the intoxicating fragrances of Mom's kitchen on Friday afternoons. When we came home from school, we went straight for the kitchen counters. Although it took much work and many hours to make all these foods, and although Mom had prepared them specifically for our Sabbath meals— she never once told us to limit our intake on Friday afternoons. Rather, she beamed with pleasure at our enthusiasm. She would say: "salud y beraha," eat with health and blessing.

Years later, when Gilda and I started to cook these foods ourselves, we realized how painstaking and time-consuming it was to prepare them. Gilda once worked for hours to make two dozen spinach boulemas for Shabbat lunch. As soon as she took them out of the oven, we and our children rushed for them. It took little time for us to finish them all off; we had none left for Shabbat lunch!

I called Mom and told her our experience. I asked: "how did you ever let us eat our fill on Friday afternoons, and still have enough for Shabbat?" She answered simply: "I always made twice as much of everything that I thought we would need for Shabbat. That way, you could eat to your heart's content on Friday and there would still be plenty for Shabbat. Salud y beraha."

For Friday night dinner, Mom would normally prepare a first course of fish—usually salmon, fixed in a sweet and sour tomato sauce or in a white sauce made of egg and lemon. The main course would include roasted chicken and many side dishes such as stuffed tomatoes, onions and/or green peppers; a baked dish made of macaroni and chopped meat; string beans; Spanish rice;

okra or cauliflower cooked in a sweet and sour tomato sauce; baked potatoes and sweet potatoes; stuffed grape leaves. Mom also would serve a large fresh salad, dressed simply with mayonnaise, and sometimes also flavored with parsley or mint freshly picked from our garden.

This general menu was followed each week without fail. Who could complain? The food was delicious and plentiful. It contained a wide variety of textures, colors and tastes. Who could become bored with it? No one in our family, least of all Mom, ever considered the need to vary the Friday night Sabbath dinner menu. If it had worked well for so long, why experiment with change?

But the crisis was bound to come. And it did.

One Friday night, my brother Bill suddenly raised a previously unthinkable question: "Why are we in a rut? Why do we have to eat the same thing every Friday night? Why can't we eat regular food like everyone else?"

A profound, brooding silence followed. We were shocked.

At the time of this eventful Friday night dinner, Bill was attending University of Washington. In his educational and cultural progress, he came to the conclusion that our family was old-fashioned. We did not adapt enough to modern American society. Rather, we continued to live in many ways as though we were still residing in Turkey, or as though we were new immigrants in Seattle. The food on Friday night was only a symbol of a deep-rooted traditionalism, an inability or reluctance to change or to experiment with new ways of doing things. Bill's complaint about the menu was really a reflection of a much bigger problem that was troubling him.

Mom understood the import of Bill's question. Very diplomatically, and without appearing the least bit hurt, she asked him what he would prefer to eat for Shabbat dinner. He answered: "Why can't we have steaks and potatoes? Why do we have to be in a rut?"

Before anyone could say a thing, Mom said enthusiastically: "Bill, you are right. Next week, we'll have steaks and potatoes on Friday night. There's no sin in changing our menu once in a while."

The next Friday evening, Mom kept her word. After the first course of fish, she served a wonderful dinner of steaks and potatoes. All of us loved steaks and potatoes. But on Friday night, the dinner seemed all wrong. Bill ate with gusto, whether real or feigned I do not know. The rest of us were unenthusiastic about dinner. I remember sitting at my place playing with the steak with my knife and fork. Finally, Dad said: "steaks and potatoes are delicious—but not on Friday nights. Steaks and potatoes taste like weekdays, not Shabbat."

Bill was flustered. "What can I say? You're all in a rut. You can't shake old habits." Finally, with a sense of resignation, he said: "I guess it's okay to have the regular Shabbat food if that's what everyone likes. At least we did try an experiment."

Next Friday night, and for all the Friday nights thereafter as long as Mom was well enough to cook, the traditional foods were served. No more steaks and potatoes; no other innovations; and no more complaints.

Papoo and Nona liked Birch Bay, a lazy resort town in upstate Washington. The beach was rocky, the water ice cold. The one road that ran through town had a speed limit of 10 miles per hour and there was very little traffic.

Birch Bay was a place where there was not that much to do. That was the way Papoo and Nona liked it. It was quiet, scenic, and peaceful.

Each summer, they rented a waterfront cabin for one or two weeks. Uncle Dave Romey, who usually returned to Seattle for summers, did the driving for them and stayed with them in their cabin. Our family rented a cabin next door. Uncle Dave and

Aunty Esther Amon and family rented in the same cabin complex. Sometimes, others of the extended family also arranged to spend their vacation in Birch Bay at the same time. Uncle Jack and Aunty Regina eventually bought one of the cabins and enjoyed it for many years.

As a child, I thought Birch Bay was very distant from Seattle. (It is actually only about 110 miles away.) Our trips there used to take six hours and more.

We left early Sunday morning, all the cars meeting at my grandparents' house on 15th Avenue. The car trunks were checked to be sure that nothing had been forgotten. Aside from clothes, we also packed kosher meat, bread and other kosher food items that were not available in Birch Bay. Each family also brought two sets of pots and pans, silverware, dishes—one set for meat foods and one for dairy, as is prescribed by the Jewish laws of kashrut.

Of course, everyone brought food for lunch. Since we also would make various road stops along the way, and since each stop entailed having cahve (pronounced kah-veh)—we also had provisions of thermoses of coffee and lots of home-baked pastries. Although we generally took these vacation trips in August, we also had to pack warm clothes and winter jackets; the weather in Birch Bay could turn cold or rainy. Papoo insisted that the trunk of each car had to be equipped with a rope, as well as with a warm sweater for each member of the family. Papoo followed the motto: "Be prepared."

Uncle Dave Romey, driving his 1949 Nash, led the caravan. The other cars lined up behind and our procession began. The trip to Birch Bay was not just a way to get from one place to another. It was also a reflection of a philosophy of life. The family viewed the trip as an integral part of the vacation. Uncle Dave was forever studying maps. Whenever he found what might be a "scenic spot," he had no hesitation to pull off the main road and travel many miles out of the way in order to discover this natural wonder.

We hardly traveled thirty miles and we already were at our first rest stop for cahve: Forest Park in Everett. We visited the zoo, played in the park, admired the scenery, ate a snack, and then returned to our traveling. Uncle Dave might also take another detour to Wenberg State Park. This was also just a "rest stop," although we had only traveled another twenty miles or so from Everett. Even though Wenberg was well off the main road, we did not mind; we enjoyed a quick swim, more refreshments, and then got back on the road.

No trip to Birch Bay would be complete unless we drove on the "world famous Chuckanut Drive," a marvelously scenic mountain road. We stopped along the way at Rosario Park, and perhaps one or two other picnic areas. We played baseball, ran races, threw rocks into the water, and ate a late lunch. Then we continued our voyage to Birch Bay, where we generally arrived toward evening.

No sooner had we settled in our cabins than it was dinner time. The fact that we had eaten five or six times on the road did not factor into our appetites. We were always starving upon arrival at Birch Bay. The men set up the barbeque grills as the women unpacked the food and utensils. We ate in the back yard of the cabins, right along the beach. We watched the sun set as we ate our fill.

During the week or two of vacation, we enjoyed swimming, bicycle riding, scouring the beach for snail shells, rocks and driftwood. Some of the family went horseback riding, renting horses from a nearby stable. On Shabbat, we all dressed up in nice Sabbath clothes. We gathered in Nona and Papoo's cabin for the prayer services. Our Shabbat activities consisted of long walks and long naps.

Uncle Dave felt that it was important to explore whatever scenic sites were in the vicinity. We would drive to Peace Arch Park in Blaine, right on the border between the United States and Canada. Papoo would only refer to this park by its original name, Sam Hill Park. He did not accept the designation of Peace Arch Park, feeling that it did an injustice to the memory of Sam Hill about whom Papoo knew nothing. "I don't care who Sam Hill was. If they named this park after him, then they can't take it away from him."

We would also often venture up to Vancouver for a day, being sure to stop at several "scenic spots" that Uncle Dave wanted us to see. His explorer instincts enabled us to visit the Indian reservation on Lummi Island, an Air Force base, a giant tree with a massive hole in the middle of its trunk, large enough for a car to drive through…and many other interesting sites.

In the evenings, we would go to the amusement park in the center of town. We went on rides, played games of chance where we tried to win halintrankas. Another evening activity was to search for crickets that were chirping away inside our cabin. Crickets are fine ventriloquists and it took time to learn how to outsmart them. We caught them in jars and tossed them outside. Undoubtedly, they found their way right back into the cabin because the sound of the crickets continued unabated.

Uncle Dave took it upon himself to take home movies of our travels in order to preserve our adventures for posterity. Mom used to say that he was "creative" since many of the movies turned out to be a series of blurs, flashes and bright colors. He was also known to photograph argyle socks in order to add color to the movies; he sometimes held his camera sideways or upside down, a technique that certainly added to our enjoyment when viewing the films later.

On some years, our family would spend one week in Birch Bay and another week at Seaside, Oregon. Sometimes Uncle Dave and Aunty Esther Amon and family would join us there as well. In 1956, Dad took his longest vacation from work—three weeks. We drove to Los Angeles and spent time with our relatives there, also taking in all the major tourist attractions.

One summer, while we were in Birch Bay, someone in the family said something remarkable: why do we come to Birch Bay every year? Why can't we think of other places to go on vacation? The general response was: why shouldn't we come to Birch Bay each summer? We enjoy it. The dissident was silenced for the moment, but the challenge seeped into the minds of the family. After so many happy years at Birch Bay, we started to find fault with it. The seeds of discontent had been planted.

Papoo was a traditionalist but he had a remarkably open spirit. He was not afraid to face challenges. Before the next summer arrived, Papoo asked Uncle Dave to find another location for our vacation.

Uncle Dave came up with a suggestion: Orcas Island. He pointed out the resort on his well-worn map. Orcas Island, one of the San Juan Islands in Puget Sound, could be reached by taking a ferry from Anacortes. Uncle Dave assured us that Orcas Island was "scenic and quiet." Papoo gave the go ahead; reservations were made.

The Sunday morning of vacation arrived and our caravan began in front of Nona and Papoo's house. Uncle Dave proudly led the procession and reassured us that we were in for a special adventure. Some family members were growling that we should have gone to Birch Bay; others were excited at trying a new place.

Uncle Dave kept us on schedule since we had to catch a ferry to Orcas Island. Our traditional rest stops for cahve were curtailed to two or three. We did catch the ferry and we arrived in Orcas Island for the first time in our lives. Indeed, it was scenic. And it was quiet. Uncle Dave beamed with satisfaction.

We then arrived at the complex of cabins where we were to stay for the week. When we entered our cabin, the first thing that struck us was a very pungent odor. The second thing that struck us was that the cabin did not have a bathroom. After some searching, we found an outhouse in the back of the cabin. It smelled so bad that I refused to enter it. Dad told me: "I don't blame you for not wanting to go in to the outhouse. But when you've got to go you've got to go." I pursed my lips and assured him that I was not going into that outhouse for the entire week, no matter what.

Mom realized that things had not gotten off to a great start. She decided that a cup of coffee would help set things straight. She put the coffee pot on the gas burner and turned the flame to its highest setting. The flames were so high that they literally reached the handle of the coffee pot. In spite of the prodigious fire, after a half hour the water in the coffee pot was still cold.

All the other families in our group had similar experiences. Dad told Uncle Dave that Orcas Island was not for us, that we ought to head for Birch Bay. Why waste the precious week of vacation in such unpleasant conditions? Uncle Dave smiled knowingly. He assured Dad and the rest of us that Orcas Island was a paradise, a splendid, scenic and quiet resort. Dad was not to be convinced: "Maybe it's good for fishermen, but it is not good for us." Papoo interjected: "Some people got tired of Birch Bay and wanted to try something new. So this is something new. No one should complain."

We all went back to our cabins and sulked.

By dinner time, Mom and Dad had decided that our family was not going to stay the week in Orcas Island. The facilities were primitive, the stench was palpable, the stove didn't heat up the food, and I would not use the outhouse under any circumstances. We didn't even unpack our things. Dad assured us that we would leave on the 9 am ferry the next morning and find a cabin in Birch Bay.

This decision having been made, Dad went to Papoo's cabin to inform him of our plans to leave in the morning. Papoo called a family meeting and announced our decision. Everyone else immediately agreed with us—let's leave as soon as possible! Papoo turned to Uncle Dave: "What do you say, Dave? Orcas Island was your discovery." Uncle Dave, ever the gentleman, announced that he was prepared to follow the decision of the majority, though he felt we had not given Orcas Island enough of a chance. Papoo stated: "It is decided. We will leave for Birch Bay on the morning ferry. Everyone be ready on time. If we miss that ferry, there is not another one until the next day."

A glow of happiness burst out among all the family. We were leaving. We were going to our beloved Birch Bay.

The next morning, we put our things in the trunk of the car and prepared to leave. Mom noticed that the meat that had been stored in the freezer compartment of the refrigerator had not frozen. The freezer obviously did not work. This meant that our entire week's supply of kosher meat was in danger of spoiling—

and it was only Monday.

Well, if worse came to worse, we could share the meat that the other families had brought. We soon learned, though, that all their meat had also thawed out overnight.

"Don't worry," Uncle Dave wisely suggested, "we'll stop at a state park on the way to Birch Bay and we can barbeque all the meat. That way it won't spoil." No one could come up with a better idea, so Uncle Dave's plan was adopted.

Our cars started on the way to the ferry boat. We already were running a bit late, and everyone was anxious not to miss the ferry. Surprisingly, Uncle Dave—driving the lead car—pulled off the road into the parking lot of a grocery store. Dad, who was driving the car right behind Uncle Dave, called out the window. "Dave, what's the problem? We're got to hurry to catch the ferry otherwise we'll be stuck here another day."

Smiling, Uncle Dave raised three coke bottles. "I bought these yesterday, and I want to return the bottles for the deposit."

"Get back into your car," Dad hollered. "I'll pay you for the bottle deposits myself."

So Uncle Dave returned to his driver's seat and we were off. We arrived at the ferry with about thirty seconds to spare.

The ferry landed at Anacortes, and Uncle Dave suggested that the best place for our barbeque was Deception Pass, not far away. Once we arrived, all the meat was unpacked and barbeques were set up. The women and girls brought the meat to the grills, and the men and boys watched it cook. No sooner had the grills been cleared of one batch of meat, the next batch was put on. We ate to contentment—and then some. Amazingly, the entire week's supply of meat was barbequed that day, and all of it was eaten right then. The women were worried that if all the meat were eaten now, there would be none left for the rest of the week including Shabbat. But seeing that everyone was having such a good time, the women agreed with Nona who said "salud y beraha, let everyone eat in good health and blessing." And we did.

The only meat that remained after our picnic were a few salamis. These were saved for Sabbath meals. The rest of the week we ate fish and vegetable dishes.

When we arrived in Birch Bay, we were fortunate to find enough cabins for all of our families and we enjoyed the rest of vacation together. As we sat on the beach that night watching the glorious sunset, Dad asked Uncle Dave: "So, Dave, what did we learn from our adventure in Orcas Island?" Uncle Dave replied with a wan smile on his face: "If you have something you like, you should stick with it. You shouldn't feel dissatisfied." Papoo added: "That's true. But a person has to be ready to try new things too. Sometimes they work out, and sometimes they don't."

But we never again veered from Birch Bay for vacation with Papoo and Nona.

Mom used to say somewhat in jest: "I don't have friends, I only have relatives." The fact was that life did revolve around the extended family. Most of our relatives lived in the same neighborhood, within easy walking distance of each other. It was usual for us to visit the homes of our uncles and aunties and for them to visit us. No invitations were necessary.

Nona and Papoo firmly believed that the family had to stay together. They had both come to Seattle as teenagers, uprooted from their parents' homes in Turkey. They knew what family life had been in the old country and they wanted to transplant the old traditions in Seattle. On one level, their lives in Seattle represented a radical break with their past; yet, in their own minds, they were symbols of continuity.

A basic feature of their traditionalism was religion. They maintained a kosher home and expected their children to do likewise when they married. They observed the Sabbath and holidays without fail, and expected their children to follow their pattern.

We were together with family on happy occasions. We grew up

with the feeling that life is good, that religion is joyful, that family is dependable. Papoo could see, though, that the hold of religion within the community was weakening.

Men of his generation struggled to make their livings; many found it necessary to work on the Sabbath. At first, they felt guilty about desecrating the Sabbath. Soon, though, they came to justify their behavior: this is America, not Turkey. The rules of life have changed and we must change too. Should we starve ourselves and our families by not working on Saturday? Many of the immigrant generation learned to violate the Sabbath; they even learned to overcome feelings of guilt about it. If the immigrants who had grown up as Sabbath observers were now abandoning Sabbath observance, what could be expected of their children and grandchildren who never saw the Sabbath properly observed?

One Shabbat morning, we began our walk home after synagogue services. It was raining heavily. One of the older men of the community drove by in his car and saw our family group getting drenched in the rain. He certainly knew that it was forbidden to ride in a car on Shabbat, and he also knew that our family observed Shabbat as carefully as we could. Yet, he pulled his car next to us, opened his window, and called out: "Can I give you a lift home?"

We thought he was brazen. It was bad enough that he was transgressing the laws of Shabbat. Didn't he at least have enough shame not to flaunt his sin before us?

Papoo's countenance was stern. He tried not to look the man in the face. He pulled his raincoat closer around his neck and continued to walk. We all followed him. The man in the car honked at us as he drove off. He shouted: "I pity you."

Papoo huddled our family together as we stood in the hard rain. "I pity him," Papoo said. "We will get wet today but we will remain pure in the eyes of God." The Talmud teaches that it is better to be thought a fool in this world than ever to do anything foolish in the eyes of God.

We didn't mind getting soaked that Shabbat. Papoo had made

us feel proud.

Papoo cared about our religious upbringing and sought to convey his strong feelings to us on various occasions. I was once invited to a friend's Bar Mitzvah that was taking place at Herzl, a Conservative synagogue just a few blocks from the Sephardic Bikur Holim building. My parents allowed me to attend, as a courtesy to my friend. Papoo was not pleased. I explained to him that I was only going to Herzl this one time in honor of my friend; no harm would come to me if I went there just this once.

"That is what everyone thinks," said Papoo. "They imagine they will do something only once and no harm will come to pass. Sometimes this is true. But often enough, one time leads to another, one sin drags another behind. It is the beginning of unravelling the rope."

I assured Papoo I would not allow myself to be tainted by the experience. He put out his hand; I kissed it. He blessed me and sent me on my way. "Remember," he told me, "stay faithful to our tradition. Those who break with tradition destroy themselves and their families."

I attended the Bar Mitzvah. After services at Herzl, I went to the Sephrdic Bikur Holim where services ended at about the same time. I met Papoo as he was leaving the synagogue. He looked me in the eye: "Remember," he said.

"I will," I responded. And I did.

Growing up in our family and community, our lives were strongly impacted by the rhythms of the Jewish holy days. Many of those childhood memories have remained with me to this day.

On the Sunday mornings before Rosh haShanah, the New Year, it was customary to hold penitential services known as selihot. These services, which began at 4 a.m., were usually held in the homes of various members of the community.

Dad used to take my brother Bill and me to selihot at the home of Uncle Solomon and Aunty Sarah. A group of twenty or thirty men gathered there, crowding into the living room. As the men chanted the penitential prayers in Hebrew and Ladino, Aunty Sarah was busy in the kitchen preparing breakfast for all who attended. To this day, when I hear a melody from the selihot service, I can smell the aroma of sweet rolls being baked, and the fragrance of strong percolated coffee.

At one of the selihot breakfasts, the conversation turned to the language of our prayers. One of the "progressive" men suggested that some of the prayers should be recited in English. After all, many of the men did not understand Hebrew. Many of the younger men and children did not understand Ladino. Why not say some of the prayers in English so that everyone can understand?

This suggestion led to a heated controversy. Some agreed with the suggestion, others just nodded their heads as they ate their sweet rolls and drank their coffee. Others were outraged by the suggestion and let everyone know it. Papoo listened to everyone patiently and then made his own comments. Hebrew is our sacred language. Ladino has acquired a kind of sanctity by virtue of its being used for prayer by generations of our ancestors. English has no holiness for us. It is better to recite prayers in Hebrew without understanding them, rather than to say them in English. Prayers mean more than their words. Prayers are sacred, they link us with God and with our ancestors. If anyone wants to know what the Hebrew words mean, he can read the English translation on his own. If we do not pray in the language of our ancestors, it is not real prayer.

With Papoo's remarks, the "progressives" became silent.

On Rosh haShana and Passover, our extended family was too large to meet in one place. Uncle Solomon and Aunty Sarah and family would be together with Uncle Jack and Aunty Regina and family. (Aunty Sarah and Aunty Regina, my mother's sisters, married two brothers, Jack and Solomon Maimon.) Aunty Estreya and Uncle Vic and family would be with members of Uncle Vic's family. Our family, Uncle Leo and Aunty Florence and family, Uncle Dave and Aunty Esther and family, and Uncle Dave Romey would be at Nona and Papoo's.

Papoo presided at these meals. On Rosh haShana he led in the special yehi ratsones, blessings over symbolic foods, praying for a sweet and happy year filled with abundance, peace and security. On Pessah, he presided over the Seder on both nights. Papoo insisted that each member of the family participate in the recitation of the Haggada, whether in Hebrew, Ladino or English. Papoo allowed English since the Haggadah is not in the category of prayer. Rather, it is a study text recounting the Exodus from Egypt. When it comes to study, Papoo felt that people should use a language that they understood. Yet, most of the men stayed with Hebrew and Ladino.

On the night when the Passover festival ended, Papoo and the men of the family remained in the synagogue for a few minutes after services. The children were home with Nona and the women. Nona gave each of the children a brown paper bag. And then the wait began.

All of us children were in a state of heightened anticipation. The older ones teased the younger ones. The younger ones peered out the windows to see if Papoo and the men were coming. There would inevitably be knocks on the back door. All of us would run excitedly to the kitchen. There was no one there; it was only a trick on us. Then there would be knocking at the front door and we rushed to the front hall. Another false alarm. At last the knocking on the door would really be Papoo and the men. The door would be opened quickly, and Papoo tossed a fistful of coins onto the floor. The children scrambled to get the money. Then the other men threw coins and candy, mixed with long blades of grass. The money throw continued throughout the living room and dining room area. The older children went for the coins, the younger ones went for the candies. The women saw to it that all the children succeeded. If the older children were blocking out the younger ones, the women would drop coins right in front of the younger ones so they could not miss getting some for themselves.

This custom symbolized the Israelites crossing the Red Sea during their exodus from Egypt. The grass was reminiscent of the reeds the Israelites experienced at the sea. The coins were reminders that the Egyptians had given gold and silver to the Israelites when the slaves left their servitude; the candies symbolized the manna that the Israelites ate upon entering the wilderness.

During the course of the "money throw," the men sang a traditional song in Ladino. Afterwards, the children counted up their loot. Every face was filled with joy. Every heart was glad. Judaism was a happy, joyous way of life.

Our lives were marked by the regular rhythms of Shabbat and holidays; but also by the events of the life cycle. In a large extended family, there were many occasions that entailed a religious or communal component i.e. circumcisions, baby namings, Bar Mitzvahs (there were no Bat Mitzvahs in our synagogues in those days), birthdays, graduations, engagements, weddings, anniversaries…and on the other end of the pendulum, funerals, mourning periods, death anniversaries. The common denominator of these observances was food.

During the early years of my childhood, the women of the family would get together to cook and bake for these special occasions. The older women, born in the old country, taught their daughters and nieces the traditional recipes and manner of preparation. They showed how to make fila dough, stretching it paper thin over tables, working quickly so the dough would not become brittle. They assigned children the task of grinding the nuts that would be part of the filling for the baklava, a honey-drenched pastry made with the fila dough. While some women worked on the baklava, others were preparing a variety of cookies and pastries. Another group would be making marzipan cookies, using home-prepared almond paste. Depending on the nature of the occasion to be celebrated and the number of people who were expected to attend, these baking sessions might take a day or two, or be spread over several weeks.

During these cooking sessions, the generations of women in the family worked together, gossiped, and sang traditional Ladino songs. They personified the continuity and vitality of the old-world culture brought to Seattle from Turkey and Rhodes.

In the early 1960s, commercially made fila dough and almond paste became available at some of the specialty stores. Most of the women quickly switched to the store-bought ingredients, saving themselves numerous hours of labor. Although everyone agreed that the commercially produced ingredients were not as good as the home made, expedience prevailed over traditionalism. It now became less necessary for the women to get together for cooperative baking. One woman could now make baklava and marzipan pastries on her own, without needing help from anyone else. Time was gained; but an element of family solidarity was lost in the process.

Mothers taught their daughters how to run a kosher home. They also added some traditions that they had learned from their own mothers. For example, it was not permitted to cook meat in its own juices; oil had to be put in the pan before placing the meat in it. Also, it was mandatory for a cook to give a sample of the food to one who had smelled it while it was cooking and expressed a desire to taste it. Otherwise, the person would have an unfulfilled longing in the soul. When a person ate to contentment, the hostess should say salud y beraha, health and blessing.

While most of the family observances centered around joyful events, some were related to sad times. After funerals, the mourners would return home from the cemetery and eat a traditional mourners' meal of bread and hard boiled eggs. Family members, neighbors and friends prepared all the meals for the mourners during the seven-day mourning period. They not only prepared enough for the mourners, but they cooked enough for guests who would be paying visits during meal times.

Among our Sephardic customs is the meldado, a study session held on the anniversary of the death of a loved one. I well remember the meldados observed in my childhood home and in the homes of relatives. Family and friends would gather in the hosts' homes. Prayer services were held. Passages from the Talmud (Mishnayot) were read. The rabbi would share words of Torah. The event evoked a spirit of family and communal solidarity, solemnity, reminiscing. But meldados were not sad occasions! After the prayers and study, there was an abundance of food prepared by the hostess. People ate, and chatted, and laughed. People would remember stories about the deceased person whose meldado was being observed, drawing on the good and happy memories. The memorialized person would have wanted family and friends to celebrate, to remember him or her with happiness and laughter.

Once people began to move out of the old neighborhood, things changed. People moved to bigger homes in nicer districts. The family and community was spread out over a wider area. Many of the observances that used to take place in homes were gradually relocated to the synagogues. Some of the traditionalists insisted on keeping these observances at home; but the tide was turning, and could not be reversed.

Progress came at a cost.

Part V

Changing Neighborhoods, Changing Lives

Uncle Dave Romey was the only one of my parents' siblings to have attended college. He had served in the American armed forces during World War II and was one of the many who benefitted from the government's programs to subsidize college expenses for veterans. He studied Spanish language and literature at the University of Washington, and was especially interested in the Spanish roots of the Sephardic Jews in Seattle. His Master's dissertation on the culture of Seattle's Sephardim was a significant scholarly contribution, making him one of the pioneers in the field of Sephardic studies in the United States. Several other Sephardic university students in Seattle—Albert Adatto and Emma Adatto—also wrote dissertations on the history and culture of Seattle's Sephardim. These dissertations by American-born Sephardim reflected love for their tradition, but also an awareness that the old Sephardic culture was undergoing a serious and permanent transformation.

Nona and Papoo and their generation spoke Judeo-Spanish naturally and unselfconsciously. They saw no need to analyze or study their language or civilization. The young people of the next generation, though deeply steeped in the Ladino traditions,

131

were already becoming Americanized. Their main language was English. They sang American songs, danced to American music, told American stories. Ladino was used almost exclusively in their conversations with members of the immigrant generation.

Uncle Dave realized that a cultural transformation was underway. The more he devoted himself to Ladino, the more he recognized that the culture was slipping away. He never wanted to admit the inevitability of this process; but he was far too insightful not to understand what was happening. He was a staunch traditionalist; yet he wanted to find ways of keeping the tradition alive among the new generations for whom Ladino was no longer the mother-tongue.

One of Uncle Dave's distinctive contributions to our family's life was his use of Ladino proverbs in English form. For example, if he ate something delicious, he complimented the cook by saying: "one b. one d." This was short for the Ladino saying, un bocado un ducado, one bite of the food is worth one gold ducat. To describe an individual whose personality traits never seemed to improve, Uncle Dave would say: "from eight to eighty." This was the English translation of the Ladino proverb, de los ocho fina los ochenta. A person's traits are established by age eight and do not change even by age eighty. A snoopy person was described as a spoon, cuchara, since a spoon stirs up the pot and checks on all the ingredients. A bland person was one "who did not go down with salad," no basha ni con salata, i.e. was unpalatable even when accompanied by something good. People who were on uneasy terms were "friends like a cat and dog," amigos como el perro y el gato. If Uncle Dave said that he had parsley growing on his nose, he was alluding to the proverb fuyi del prexil me crecio en la nariz, I ran from the parsley, it grew on my nose. This meant that one did not escape that which he was trying to escape. We all came to use Uncle Dave's Anglicized Ladino sayings. In one sense, we were maintaining the old traditions; but in another sense we were transforming those traditions into American terms.

Most Sephardim of Uncle Dave's generation could not afford the luxury of attending college. He was the first member of our community to become a teacher in a university, and his intellectual achievements were a source of pride to our family. He taught Spanish at the University of Vermont, Temple University, Drew University, and then spent many years teaching at Portland State University. Much of his early career was spent "back East," much to the distress of Nona. Whenever he was returning to Seattle for Passover or for summer vacation, our entire family gathered at Nona and Papoo's house for a party. Whenever he had to return to his college, we all met again at their house for a somber farewell gathering. Nona was terrified of airplanes (and never traveled on one), and she dreaded Uncle Dave's need to travel by air. After Uncle Dave had left for the airport, Nona would sob for hours until she received a call from him informing her that he had landed safely.

Mom spoke of Uncle Dave with love and reverence, seeing in him an educational fulfillment that she herself had never experienced. Although Mom was quite well-read and an intellectual in her own right, she always deferred to her brother Dave since he was a "genuine scholar."

Whereas only a few Sephardim were able to attend university in Uncle Dave's generation, by the 1950s almost all Sephardim of college age were attending college. Most attended the University of Washington in Seattle. My cousin Al was one of the few Sephardim who went to school out of town, attending Yeshiva College in New York City. After receiving his BA degree, he attended law school at the University of Washington. Al was the first born of Mom's older sister Regina. He, like Uncle Dave, was a religious loyalist, and brought pride to the family as our first attorney.

Al and a number of others of similar traditionalist bent were in the minority. Most Sephardic college students of his generation were moving away from the old patterns of Sephardic life. The process of acculturation that had already begun in the immigrant generation began to accelerate. Even those who grew up in the more traditionalist families were changing their ways. Sabbath observance declined. The dietary laws were compromised or abandoned altogether.

No longer was it assumed that the wisdom of the older generations was valid for the new generation in America. College professors became the new authorities; peer pressure became a major molder of values. Some parents, who were themselves not college educated, began to defer authority to their college trained children. Some parents battled with their children, trying to keep them in line. Others looked the other way, hoping that the rebelliousness of their children was just a passing phase, and that they would return to the normal patterns once they married and had families of their own.

Many of the young Sephardim were marrying spouses who were not Sephardic, or who were not Jewish. It could no longer be assumed that wedding receptions would be kosher, nor that the young couples would maintain kosher homes. Young couples now started to move to the suburbs, especially Mercer Island and Bellevue.

The community was showing signs of breakdown. No oppressor forced the people to give up their traditions. No one threatened them to leave the Jewish neighborhood. They were doing it to themselves of their own free will.

They had a name for their behavior: progress. Uncle Dave also had a name for it: spiritual and cultural suicide.

Russell, our next door neighbor on 28th Avenue, moved away in 1957. The neighborhood was already in the midst of change. More and more blacks were moving in; more and more whites were moving out.

Russell, a hard-working and dignified man, was himself a black. He had been our neighbor for many years. His son, Jerome, was our friend. Russell insisted that his son be called Jerome, not Jerry. Jerome was kept neatly dressed and was taught to be respectful and courteous.

When Jerome was old enough to be enrolled in school, Russell did not want him to go to Horace Mann, the elementary public school on 25th Avenue, just across the street from the Jewish Day School. Horace Mann was a troubled "inner city" school and Russell wanted his son in a more genteel setting with a proper educational atmosphere. Russell enrolled Jerome in the elementary school in the neighboring Madrona district, believing that this would be a better place for him.

The first months at Madrona were terrifying for Jerome. He came home crying each day. Kids picked on him, beat him up. He was frightened to go to school. Seeing Jerome's distress, Russell managed to get him transferred to a school in another district, Leschi. Jerome stopped complaining about school; but he also changed. He insisted on being called Jerry. His face hardened. He started to use foul language. He refused to dress neatly. He talked back to his father. At Leschi, Jerry had become a tough, ill-mannered boy. My brother David and I spent less and less time with Jerry.

In 1957, Russell sold his house and moved to the other side of town. "They drove me out," he told Dad. "They're destroying my son. I've got to get away from here before it's too late."

Russell was not the first of our neighbors to move out. Some said they were leaving because they had more money now and they wanted to live in nicer areas. Others said they were moving to get away from the deterioration that was engulfing our neighborhood. Some said they had to move because they were afraid to stay.

Our old neighborhood was changing for the worse. The house across the street from us was now occupied by several women with numerous little children. Different men showed up from time to time, but never seemed to stay very long. The noise level in the neighborhood went up. Some of the new neighbors did not tend their lawns or keep their houses painted properly. Crime increased. Neighborhood store owners were experiencing vandalism and theft. Our world was coming apart in front of our eyes. Inexorably. Without anyone able to reverse the trend.

Our synagogue, Ezra Bessaroth, came to the conclusion that the congregation would have to sell its building on 15th Avenue and build a new synagogue in the Seward Park area where some members had already relocated. A vocal minority of traditionalists argued against the move. We had been praying in our synagogue building for many years and we liked it here. If we all decided not to move out of this neighborhood, we could maintain our present building and keep our congregation going here. Our families have been living in this neighborhood since the Sephardic immigrants had first arrived from Turkey and Rhodes. We had a lot of good memories here, a sense of togetherness and continuity.

But the move to Seward Park was necessary. The synagogue on 15th Avenue would be unable to sustain itself much longer. The congregation voted to sell the current building and erect a new one on the corner of Wilson Avenue South and South Brandon Street. There was a gap of over a year between the time of the sale of the old synagogue and the building of a new facility. During the interim, members of Ezra Bessaroth worshipped at Sephardic Bikur Holim on 20th and Fir or at other synagogues. For the High Holy Days, the congregation rented a hall where services were conducted according to its custom. Meanwhile, members who were still living in the old neighborhood made plans to move to the area where the new synagogue was being built.

Dad accepted the inevitability of the move to Seward Park. In fact, he was eager to relocate our family there. Homes in Seward Park were newer and larger. Since the old neighborhood was declining seriously, it was surely time to move a better, safer neighborhood.

Mom, though, had a different point of view. Under no circumstances did she want to move from 511 28th Avenue. This was the home where she had lived since 1940, where she had raised her children. This home was in walking distance of her parents' home and her sisters' homes. Even if Ezra Bessaroth had decided to move, Sephardic Bikur Holim was staying in the neighborhood. There was still a group of traditionalists who resisted moving to the new area.

Dad thought that he could persuade Mom by offering reasonable arguments: our family deserves to be in a better home in a better neighborhood; moving to Seward Park won't prevent you from visiting your parents and sisters and other relatives. He convinced her to take driving lessons so she would be able to drive to the old neighborhood whenever she wanted.

Mom was deeply distraught. Why should we allow others to drive us out of our own home, out of our own neighborhood? If we all stay, we can keep things stable.

But everyone was not staying. Many were selling their homes as soon as they could. Like it or not, the neighborhood as we had known it was coming apart. Friends and relatives moved away; strangers moved in. Well-established stores closed. The streets became increasingly dangerous and crime-ridden.

A gang of hoodlums got into a knife fight in front of Aunty Sarah's house on 26th Avenue. One of the victims bled on her front steps and porch. The sons of new neighbors climbed into Aunty Regina's yard and stole cherries from her trees. Cousins playing baseball in a public field were accosted by a group of teenagers who hit them and made anti-Jewish comments. A man walked into Uncle Jack's butcher shop and took a chicken for which he refused to pay. Gangs of students from Horace Mann intimidated the children of the Jewish Day School, taunting, threatening, fighting. Almost every day, there was another unpleasant incident. How much patience could we have? How much longer should we allow ourselves to be subjected to the violence and immorality all around us?

Dad convinced Mom that they should at least look at homes in the Seward Park area. Maybe she would like one of them. Mom reluctantly agreed but found fault with every home they saw. "We are better off where we are," she insisted. "Why should we move so far away?"

Dad hoped we would be living in Seward Park no later than early summer of 1958. My Bar Mitzvah was scheduled for August 2, 1958, and Dad wanted this event to be celebrated in our own synagogue, Ezra Bessaroth. Mom reminded him that the new building in Seward Park might not even be completed by that time; and even if it was, we could not have the Bar Mitzvah there because many relatives would be unable to attend. They were religiously observant and did not travel by car on the Sabbath. How were they to get to Seward Park? They could not be expected to walk the five or six miles from the old neighborhood. She thought that my Bar Mitzvah should be held at the Sephardic Bikur Holim, where her father had been a pioneer and leader, and where most of her relatives prayed.

So it was settled. I would be Bar Mitzvah at the Sephardic Bikur Holim. I began lessons with my Uncle Solomon, who was the rabbi of the Bikur Holim. Dad arranged that I prepare a speech under the direction of Rabbi Isidore Kahan of the Ezra Bessaroth. He also arranged that we would have a special celebration at the new building of Ezra Bessaroth on Sunday morning, August 3, when I would don my tefillin and make a short talk. This would be followed by a breakfast for all the guests. And so it was. I was the first boy to celebrate his Bar Mitzvah in the new building of the Ezra Bessaroth, albeit on a Sunday morning rather than on a Shabbat.

The Shabbat of my Bar Mitzvah was celebrated at the Sephardic Bikur Holim. After services, our family went to Nona and Papoo's house for lunch. Nona, whose health had been declining, was too ill to walk all the way to synagogue. When we had lunch with her, I recited some of my Bar Mitzvah speech, and she cheered me on with glee. On Saturday night, my parents arranged a reception in my honor at the Norway Center, the only hall in those days that had facilities for kosher catering. On Sunday morning, we all went to the new Ezra Bessaroth building where I participated in the services. We then had a festive breakfast for family and friends who had come to synagogue in honor of the occasion.

After my Bar Mitzvah, Dad continued to discuss with Mom the need for us to move to Seward Park. He was very sensitive to her fears and anxieties, but he was determined to win her consent. She finally liked a house that was shown to her, a block away from Ezra Bessaroth; but she was still hesitant. Finally Dad convinced her to agree to have our house on 28th Avenue put up for sale.

When the real estate agent planted a "for sale" sign in our front yard, Mom pulled it out and tossed it in the garbage. When potential buyers came to see the house, she would tell them that the house wasn't actually for sale yet. Dad was very patient, but also very persistent.

Mom was desperately trying to hold onto something. It wasn't just the house that was at risk; it was the world that the house represented. You don't just pick up a family and move away to a strange new house in a new neighborhood. You don't just leave behind relatives and friends, and the whole fabric of life of which the house was part. A house wasn't just a physical structure, it was a way of life.

Mom did not want to break with that way of life.

Mom was a stoic, self-styled martyr. Her philosophy was to accept life as it came and to make the best of things. Nevertheless, she did have a stubborn streak and did find ways to assert her ideas and interests.

She almost never cried. I remember a few times seeing her cry when she was in extreme physical pain. These displays of tears were rare, and she usually forced herself to recover quickly. The tears seemed to leave no trace on her once she overcame them.

I remember her crying deeply and uncontrollably only three times. In each of these cases, the tears never really went away. All her inner strength could not totally wash away the introduction of a new shade of melancholy.

The first time occurred when Mom had finally agreed to put

our house up for sale. A real estate agent brought a respectable looking and very cheerful husband and wife. They went from room to room and at each stop the woman expressed her satisfaction: she just loved the house, she just loved the wallpaper, she just loved the kitchen, she just loved the yard, she just loved everything about 511 28th Avenue. After their tour of our home, they were jubilant. They told the agent that they wanted to make an offer to buy the house. Mom's face stiffened and she could scarcely get words out of her mouth.

Once the agent and buyers left, Mom calmly went into her bedroom and closed the door behind her. Then she cried with all the anguish of her soul; she cried without holding anything back. I was in the living room and overheard her crying. Terrified, I went to her room to see what was wrong. I peeked in and saw her weeping. I walked in and tried to comfort her, but I found myself crying right along with her. "What's wrong, Mommy?" I sobbed.

She hugged me tightly. "We're going to have to move away from here. We're going to have to leave our house."

"But aren't we moving to a better house?" I asked.

She nodded, but kept crying.

She was crying for the end of an era. She was crying for the past that was gone, for the future that was uncertain. She was mourning a great loss in her life, in our lives.

By the time Dad got home from work that night, Mom had tried to recover her usual composure. There was a profound sadness in her eyes that she could not hide, a sadness that never fully went away.

Our house was sold. Mom and Dad had found a nice house in the Seward Park neighborhood at 5602 Wilson Avenue South. It was a large white stucco home, dramatically nicer than our home at 511 28th Avenue. Given the choice of living in either of these houses, almost anyone would choose the one on Wilson Avenue South. But Mom still had her reservations.

She had lived in the home on 28th Avenue for eighteen years. She was to live in the home on Wilson Avenue South for twenty-five years; yet, she would refer to the home in Seward Park as "the new house."

We moved to our new home in the summer of 1959. Mom took driving lessons and received her license. She would not allow herself to feel isolated from her parents and the rest of the family still living in the old neighborhood.

We knew that Mom was adjusting to the new house when she planted parsley, mint and tomatoes, just as she had done in the backyard of our old house. She also planted flowers that had grown on 28th Avenue—silver dollars and Chinese lanterns. She had Uncle Dave Amon, who was a very able gardener, transplant a plum tree from the old yard into the new one.

Mom was eager to have our rutha bush (rue) from 28th Avenue transplanted in the front yard of our house on Wilson Avenue South. The rutha bush in our old garden had grown from a cutting from the rutha bush in the yard of Nona and Papoo on 15th Avenue. Aside from giving off a strikingly pleasant fragrance, rutha was considered to be "good luck," a sure deflector of the evil eye.

Uncle Dave Amon brought cuttings from the old rutha bush and re-planted them in our new yard. He could not get the rutha to take. It would remain green for a week or so and then would fade into grey and brown as it died out. He tried to get the rutha bush going several times, but each attempt ended in failure. Mom took this as a bad omen. Uncle Dave assured her that he would try again in the spring.

Mom had other things to worry about aside from the rutha bush. Nona, whose health had been declining, had fallen seriously ill. For a while, she had been hospitalized but then was brought back home. I asked Mom if I could visit Nona. She replied: "She isn't the same Nona that you knew. She's very sick. She has tubes sticking into her. It's better for you not to see her this way. You should remember her as she was, not the way she is now."

As November approached, Mom considered what to do about the Thanksgiving holiday. For many years, she had invited the entire family to our house for Thanksgiving dinner. She felt she should do so again this year; and yet, how could we have a festive holiday meal while Nona was deathly ill? Mom concluded that we would have a small Thanksgiving dinner ourselves; she could not emotionally handle a large family gathering.

On the Saturday before Thanksgiving 1959, Nona died.

On Sunday, family and friends gathered at the Jewish funeral chapel on 12th and Alder. Our ride to the chapel had been long and quiet. Mom sat in the front seat with a stoic expression, seemingly in control of her emotions. Dad parked the car near the chapel and got out to open the door for Mom. As soon as he opened the door, Mom started to cry uncontrollably. Dad, face solemn and grieved, hugged her and tried to comfort her. She was beyond consolation. In an instant, we were all crying, not just in mourning for Nona but for the horrible grief suffered by Mom.

I have never forgotten that eternal instant of grief. Nona's death was an ending, not just of her life but of our family's pattern of life.

Mom had been adjusting slowly to the recent move to Seward Park. Now, a few months later, she was confronted with the death of her mother. Mom, the usually restrained martyr, could not withstand these cataclysmic events without crying helplessly.

The seven days of mourning passed. Autumn was ending, the Seattle winter was beginning.

In the spring, Uncle Dave Amon planted a rutha cutting in our front yard, as he had promised to do. This time it took. The cutting soon grew into a large healthy bush. Mom took this as an omen that the transition to our new lives in Seward Park would also take hold.

The third time I saw Mom cry helplessly was in February 1983 when I came in from New York to visit her in the Group Health hospital in Seattle. As I entered her room, I found her sitting on a chair in the corner. Before I could say a word, before she could say a word—she cried with the fullness of anguish that I had seen in her only twice before.

As she was crying, she reached out her hand to me: "I'm dying, Marc. I'm going to die."

My grandparents and their generation have passed away.

My parents and all their siblings have passed away.

My generation is getting on in years. Some of my cousins have died or are in declining health. Some still live in Seattle, but some live in Portland, Los Angeles, Sioux Falls, New York, Jerusalem…and other places. Some are religiously traditional, and some have moved far from Jewish religious observance.

Our children and grandchildren live in a world much removed from the "old neighborhood" in Seattle where I was born and raised. They have little contact with the children and grandchildren of the cousins of my generation. They have hardly heard (or never heard) Judeo-Spanish as a living language. They have no first hand memories of the lives of the pioneer Sephardic immigrants who came to America in the early 20th century.

Peter Berger, an eminent scholar of modern American civilization, has noted that moderns suffer from a deepening condition of spiritual "homelessness." The old anchors and moorings have not held.

The old days are gone forever. Looking back can be pleasant; but it cannot create a new framework for society. It is not enough to have a "home" in the past. We need to be at home in the present and to create homes for our children and grandchildren.

The "old country of Seattle" cannot be put back together. It is gone, never to return. But values can live on; attitudes can be transmitted; ideas can transcend time and space. Moderns need not be spiritually homeless if they can create a society based on love, trust, shared values and ideals. Our sense of being at home will come from inner strength, from our immediate family and friends, from our communal structures. For our future generations to feel that life is whole, meaningful and secure, we will need to create frameworks where they feel "at home," comfortable with themselves, comfortable with the world in which they live.

Our grandparents and parents and their generations left us a powerful legacy of memories, values and ideals. As we draw strength and wisdom from their lives, we face the present and the future with increasing confidence. We can't go home again, but neither can we ever really leave home.

BIOGRAPHY

Rabbi Marc D. Angel is Founder and Director of the Institute for Jewish Ideas and Ideals (jewishideas.org), fostering an intellectually vibrant, compassionate and inclusive Orthodox Judaism. He is Rabbi Emeritus of the historic Congregation Shearith Israel, the Spanish and Portuguese Synagogue of New York City (founded 1654), where he began serving in 1969.

Born and raised in the Sephardic community of Seattle, Washington, he went to New York for his higher education at Yeshiva University where he earned his B.A., M.S., Ph.D. and Rabbinic Ordination. He also earned an M.A. in English Literature from the City College of New York.

Author and editor of 36 books, he has written and lectured extensively on various aspects of Jewish law, history and culture. Among his books is a collection of short stories, *The Crown of Solomon and Other Stories*, published by Albion-Andalus in 2014.

Rabbi Angel is married to Gilda Angel. Their children and grandchildren live in New York, Baltimore and Teaneck.

CPSIA information can be obtained
at www.ICGtesting.com
Printed in the USA
LVHW091816230819
628744LV00003B/482/P